SUCCESS AND HAPPINESS SERIES

BOOKS 1 – 3
THE UNDERDOG
DELUSIONS OF GRANDEUR
HAPPY

MARK LLEWHELLIN

DEDICATION

This book is dedicated to the love of my life, my little miracle, Léon James Llewhellin, who I love more than anyone in the world. You are kind, thoughtful, well balanced and you are already achieving great things in your life.

You are my biggest reason for having my life in order, and staying strong in challenging times.

Words cannot describe how much I love you and how proud I am of the person you are.

This book is also dedicated to those of you who are going through challenging times.

TABLE OF CONTENTS

THE UNDERDOG

Achieving Your Dreams Against the Odds

MARK LLEWHELLIN

INTRODUCTION

So here we go with my first book. Like many things in my life, I consider it a miracle that I've written a book. When I was younger, I never thought I'd amount to anything, I wasn't the most popular kid, I wasn't the one that all the girls chased, I wasn't the brightest kid in the class, and I wasn't the athletics superstar. In fact, running the school cross country course, which was less than 2 miles, was too much for me without stopping.

When it came to athletics and cross country, I would do my best to avoid it. It wasn't that I disliked running, I hated it, and I mean hate with a passion! You'll often read in self-development books that you have to follow your passion to do well and achieve on a high level. But if there was one thing I hated with a passion, it was running.

But like many kids I had a dream, a dream that I would one day become somebody special, that one day I would achieve things that many would consider impossible.

Have you ever had a dream or a goal that you wanted to achieve and found out that there are people (yes, even friends and family) who think you've got no chance and you're stupid for thinking you want to achieve something so big?

The truth is that most people underestimate what they can achieve, they underestimate the power of the mind, and they underestimate what they can achieve when they put their minds to it.

This can limit their belief in themselves and can ultimately stop them achieving great things in their lives. So belief is important to success, but if you're anything like me or what I was like, you may not 100% believe in yourself. That's OK: all you need to do is think it's possible.

When I was thinking about what I should call this book, I thought about my life and how things have turned out for me.

There are some bits about my life which I will mention in this book, but the purpose of this book isn't to be an autobiography, but to help you on your path to achieving what you want out of your own life.

I believe that no matter what your race, gender, religion, sexuality or age, there will be something in this book for you.

As you go through this book, you will see that some of the writing is in a bold format. The reason I have done this is because I'd like you to take special note of these words.

I've read many books on self-development and they have changed my life beyond recognition.

If you want more out of life and want to live the very best life you can, not only for yourself but also for your friends and family, then read on.

What this book will hopefully give you is belief: belief in yourself to know that you can achieve big things in your life and that you can make a difference in the lives of others.

If I can achieve what was once considered impossible for me, then hopefully you'll think, "If he can do that from where he started, then I've got a chance of making my own dreams come true."

Sometimes we look at people who have achieved impressive things and we think that's just the way they are and it's probably the way they've always been. But the truth is, most of the high achievers we read or hear about have at one stage also been underdogs. They have had to battle through challenges and by applying certain principles to their life they have triumphed against the odds and achieved their dreams.

In this book I am going to be very transparent, I'll let you take a little peak into my life and hopefully you'll get one or two useful pieces of information that will help you on your journey. Sometimes people may look at me and think I never have a challenging day, maybe I brush things off easily and simply float through life. There is some truth in that and over the years I have learned certain things that have helped me to handle challenges a bit better than most people, but like you, I am still human. I have emotions, feelings and sometimes, yes, even negative thoughts. However, there are ways to bounce back quicker from setbacks, and in this book you will read about some of the techniques I have used to take me from failure to success.

There are those people who will want to tear you down and can be pretty insulting at times. Over the years, I've been referred to in various negative ways: the wrong skin colour, fat, physically unfit, mumbles (some of the children in school used to call me this as I didn't speak very clearly at times), ugly, bald, ginger (my beard), too old and too young. I've had a lot more insults than this, but I thought I'd just tell you about the kind ones.

As with the running, I can honestly say that I didn't have an initial passion for physically writing a book. Oh, sure, like many people, I want a book out, but put the work in to make it a reality... HELL NO! It takes time to write a book, and it means I have to sit down and write, which isn't my idea of fun.

In fact, I'd rather be doing what I really love, which is sitting in front of the TV and eating Ben and Jerry's Chocolate Fudge Brownie ice cream all day long. Mmmmmmmmmmm chocolate fudge brownie with hot chocolate fudge cake. My idea of heaven is eating piles of junk food, achieving loads, and having the same body that Jean-Claude Van Damme had in "Blood Sport."

I know, I know... I'm supposed to be this health and fitness expert who doesn't eat any crap and wakes up shouting "hallelujah" every morning, but it's not quite like that. I have flaws and faults, and I'm far from perfect.

When it came to producing this book, I had no ghost writer, no massive publishing house behind me and no huge marketing campaign, but I did have a dream to get a book published. Writing this book has been a similar process to when I first started running at the age of 16. I tripped, I fell back, I missed deadlines, I had setbacks and I temporarily I failed but I never gave up.

My hope for you is that you'll get something of use out of this book that can help you to achieve your dreams in life.

You may or may not know me personally, but we do have one thing in common: at some point in our lives we've been able to say... "We are The Underdogs."

CHAPTER 1

YOU ARE A MIRACLE – LIFE IS A MIRACLE

"There are only two ways to live your life. One is as though nothing is a miracle. The other is as though everything is a miracle."

– Albert Einstein

You are a walking, breathing miracle. While we are on the path to achieving our dreams and goals, it's very easy to forget how amazing we really are. We get caught up in negative thoughts: "I'm not slim enough, not fit enough, not strong enough, not rich enough, not beautiful enough, not handsome enough" – the list goes on and on.

It's only natural to want more, that's the way human beings are built. But if we forget about our own successes in life and compare ourselves to celebrities every five minutes, then we're heading down a path of being unhappy for most of our lives.

Try a little experiment with yourself, starting right now for the next 24 hours. When 24 hours is up, ask yourself the question, "Have I spent more time thinking about what I'm grateful for or have I spent more time thinking about what I haven't got? Have I spent more time wishing I could change the past, or do I spend more time thinking about the exciting possibilities for the future?" Sometimes we are so caught up in life that we continue with our daily habits and forget to stop and analyse our thoughts and our actions. Some people will go through their entire life having the same types of thoughts every day, which can lead to a pretty poor life. Our happiness depends on how we look at things, and one of my goals in this book is to help you look at things in a more positive way. Being positive won't deliver all the answers, but it will allow us to live a happier and less stressful life.

We forget the magic and beauty of what's around us.

Take your mind back to your childhood and how much fun

you had. As adults, we can take life too seriously, our ego can take over and we then stop living in the moment and enjoying ourselves. We all love achieving things and taking our lives to the next level, but if we're stressed all the time because we're chasing someone else's perception of success, then we are not truly successful. We are sacrificing our happiness just to try and look good on the outside to other people.

Yes, it's cool achieving things in life and getting recognition from people, but we need to look at the bigger picture to see if we are living truly fulfilled lives. Are you playing by your own rules or are you playing by someone else's? Are you chasing your own dream or are you chasing what others perceive as success? Success means different things to different people and we need to achieve our own definition of success to be truly happy and fulfilled in life.

CHAPTER 2

YOUR BODY IS A MIRACLE

"We celebrate our ability to create machines that move as a man; yet we take for granted the miracle that is the human body."

– David Alejandro Fearnhead

Whether you love it or hate it, your body is pretty awesome. Here's some info about you that you may or may not know. Hopefully, what you will realise is how incredible and lucky you are to have been given this miracle called life:

Unless you have lost a limb or two, you have 206 bones in your body. Incredibly, ounce for ounce, your bones have a greater pressure tolerance than steel.

Your heart beats around 100,000 times a day, that's over 35 million times a year.

A CNN report stated researchers at Rockefeller University and the Howard Hughes Institute reported that humans can distinguish between 1 trillion smells.

According to the Daily Mail, the human eye can see over 10 million different colours

According to Anne Marie Helmenstine Ph.D, if you put all the DNA molecules in your body end to end, the DNA would reach from the Earth to the Sun and back over 600 times.

Everything is made up of atoms, me, you, water, food, the device you're reading these words on, it's all made up of tiny atoms invisible to the human eye.

If you weigh roughly 70kg (154 lbs) your body is made up of approximately 7 octillion atoms. Which is obviously 7,000,000,000,000,000,000,000,000,000 or 7 billion, billion, billion. OK, maybe not so obvious to either you or me, but this simply states how complex, how genius and how precious you are.

A lot of work has gone into you. Before you even go into self-development and creating a better life for yourself, it's important to look at the work that has already gone into your body. I mention certain engineering structures in this book that have been created by geniuses, but none of these structures are designed anywhere near as impressively as you have been.

What we have already been given as human beings is phenomenal, and to create that great life for ourselves, all we need to do is put a little bit of effort in to get the icing on the cake. OK, let's be realistic here, to excel at something to a very high level we have to put a lot of effort in, but it's still not much effort compared to what you've been given for free.

Although humans have done some pretty stupid things throughout history compared with most of the species on this planet, we are pretty smart. It is estimated by leading scientific authorities that our brains have approximately 100 billion neurones.

We have between 35-48 thoughts a minute, which is approximately 50,000-70,000 thoughts a day. That's an impressive number. So ask yourself, what are those thoughts? Because your thoughts lead to actions and your actions will create your lifestyle.

It's easy for us to put ourselves down and have negative thoughts, but it's important to take a look at how clever we really are. One of the world's fastest supercomputers that had

82,944 processors took on the power of the human brain. The supercomputer never came close; it took 40 minutes to simulate only 1 second of 1% of our brain activity.

CHAPTER 3

STANDING ON THE SHOULDERS OF GIANTS

"If I have seen further than others, it is by standing upon the shoulders of giants."
– Sir Isaac Newton

When it comes down to succeeding at anything in life, we need to look at people who have already been successful at what we want to be successful at. We can avoid making a lot of mistakes by learning from other people who have already worked things out.

On 16 March 1926, American Robert Goddard launched the world's first liquid-fuelled rocket in Auburn, Massachusetts. Although Goddard was a pioneer and achieved something great, Goddard learned from other people to make his dream a reality. One of those people was British scientist Sir Isaac Newton, who came up with his 3rd Law of Motion: "For every action, there is an equal and opposite reaction" which explained the main physics of how a rocket would work.

Even though Newton was a giant in the world of science, he also learned from other people so he could achieve great things. When Newton built the first practical telescope, he would have learned from other people. When Newton and Gottfried Leibniz developed modern calculus, they both learned from other people first.

Although great inventors, physicists and scientists like Sir Isaac Newton, Galileo Galilei, Nikola Tesla, Charles Darwin, Marie Curie, Archimedes, Alexander Fleming, Thomas Edison, Stephen Hawking and Albert Einstein are all considered geniuses, they all started off with 1 + 1 and learned from other people.

Learning from people who have excelled in their field can save you weeks, months, and sometimes even years of wasted effort. If you're anything like me, you will want to achieve your goals sooner rather than later.

When I went on the Commando Course, I had put a lot of training in so I could achieve my dream of getting the Green Beret. Unfortunately, I didn't ask any Commandos for their advice on the best type of training to do, and one of the key things that I never worked on was endurance. I worked on my upper body and I was putting in a lot of runs in for training, but the runs were too short. If I knew back then what I now know, I would have done longer runs to get used to the endurance tests that would come along on the Commando Course.

As a result, my endurance was relatively weak, and I suffered far more than I would have done if I had put the proper training in.

You may not have access to high achievers on the start of your journey, but you can always read books or blogs written by someone who has done what you want to do and how they did it, or you can read biographies to learn about how they think and how they have overcome challenges in their lives.

A word of caution: there are lots of people out there who will want to give you their advice on something. They can talk with tremendous confidence and they can be very convincing, which could lead you to make a bad decision. Just because someone talks with supreme confidence about a subject, it doesn't mean they are right about it. How many people have started a business with tons of confidence and failed? And how many politicians have we seen over the years that have convinced millions of people to follow "their way" and things have ended up going badly wrong?

This is one of the reasons why I started interviewing high achievers. I wanted to learn from these people and I also wanted to share their words of wisdom so other people could learn from them too.

One of my goals is to be a successful author. Looking at my level of education and my track record with writing, most people would write me off (excuse the pun); again, I am an underdog and my chances look slim to most people. In fact, if I told certain members of my family, they would think I'm crazy and dismiss it immediately. They would look at my track record and think "the facts are, Mark hasn't achieved anything in the writing world, so he's got no chance, it's just one of his silly little dreams". But all high achievers know that the facts can be changed if your dream is big enough and you take action and the right steps towards your dream. I don't have time to waste getting involved in family disputes, it's also a negative drain on my energy so I avoid it, and just get on with trying to achieve what I want to achieve.

When it comes to writing, publishing and marketing a book, am I going to take advice from people who aren't doing well with selling books, or am I going to take advice from people who have been through what I'm going through and have come out the other end super successful? The answer is obvious; I'm going to take the advice of the super successful ones. Unfortunately, I didn't always take their advice, and guess what, it didn't turn out well for me.

Sometimes you just have to screw up and learn certain things the hard way.

When it comes to learning about writing, publishing, and marketing books, the three main podcasts I listen to are created by Steve Scott, Mark Dawson, and Joanna Penn. Not only are they all doing incredibly well with their own writing, publishing, and marketing businesses, they also have guests on their podcasts who consistently make six and sometimes seven-figure incomes through selling their books. Yes, yes it's not all about money but given the options of:

1. Making lots of mistakes vs. making few mistakes.

2. Wasting lots of time vs. being productive with my time.

3. Making very little money vs. making lots of money, it's probably best to take the latter options, because...

A. It's less stressful.

B. I get quicker results.

C. I get more freedom to do the things I want to do with my family and friends.

When you listen to experts, sometimes the advice can be confusing because there can be a difference of opinion, so there can be more than one way to be successful. But there are certain things which they all agree on, and it's vital to take that advice.

When it comes to being a successful author, most experts

agree that one or even two books aren't enough. You have to keep producing book after book, and the more books you produce, the better the results you will get. Although I've been slow in producing this book, I've already written most of the content for my second book, Delusions of Grandeur. But I know even that's not enough, so I've produced over 70 pages of another self-development book, over 30 pages of my autobiography, there's a whole load of content from my interviews that can be put into several books and I have ideas for even more.

If you want to go deeper into life, there are also people from the world of philosophy and religion who you can learn from.

Some philosophy is good and some not so good. Some religious teachings are good and some not so good. As Shakespeare said, "there is nothing either good or bad, but thinking makes it so."

Ultimately, it's down to us what we decided to believe or not believe. But if you are aiming to improve other people's lives as well as your own, you won't go far wrong.

So when you want to achieve something, whatever it is, always find someone who has the experience with the success and learn from them.

Stand on the shoulders of giants, achieve your dreams, and become a giant yourself!

Learn from giants to propel you to the next level.

CHAPTER 4

THE BRIDGE OF LIFE

"Sometimes, if you aren't sure about something, you just have to jump off the bridge and grow your wings on the way down."

– Danielle Steel

There are several different definitions for a bridge, but the main ones are:

- "A structure that is built over a road, or a chasm to allow people to cross from one side to the other."

- "Something that makes it easier to make a change from one situation to the other."

Any of us that have goals and dreams in life first think up the dream and then think, "How am I going to get from one side to the other?"

What is certain with any big goal is that there will be big challenges that lay ahead when you want to achieve them.

There will be times in your life when you're heading towards your goal and everything is great. The sun will be shining, and you can see your destination.

These are great times but savour them and enjoy them as much as you can, because at some point things will go wrong. This isn't negative thinking; this is just the way life goes: nobody sails through life without any challenges. And just like with the Golden Gate Bridge, the fog will close in and you will no longer be able to see your destination.

These times are the times of uncertainty, and they can also be the most dangerous for you. These situations occur in life not only when you're striving for a goal but also with things that are not directly linked to your goals, for example, a relationship unexpectedly ending or the death of a loved one.

These are the times when the fog can come in thick, you think you know where you are, but you can no longer see the beauty that was there before. All of a sudden you're no longer on solid ground, but you're hundreds of feet up in the air, not knowing what might hit you next.

Sometimes you may have to slow down when you are in the fog of life. Sometimes you will be going slower than you originally planned. If that happens, you will get to your destination slower than you expected, but if you keep going, you'll get there.

I missed the original launch date for this book, which was frustrating, and I felt I had not only let people down but had let myself down, too. I had been slow with getting this book published, as lots of other things were demanding my attention. But even at a slow pace, I kept on going. And sometimes that's all you need to do in life to succeed.

Building a great life, in many ways, is the same as building an impressive structure or a great bridge. It takes effort, dedication, and determination to create something strong and impressive. And when you take on a project that has never been done before, there are many people who will doubt your ability to succeed.

Just like when I set out to achieve many of my goals, the team that built the Akashi-Kaikyo Bridge had many doubters. People doubted that they could build a suspension bridge so tough and so long.

The Akashi-Kaikyo Bridge is (at the time of writing) the

pinnacle of bridge engineering. It is the longest suspension bridge in the world, with a central span of 1,991 metres and an overall length of 3,911 metres with two main supporting towers.

It can withstand typhoon winds of up to 178 mph, harsh sea currents, tsunamis and earthquakes measuring up to magnitude 8.5. It's a marvel of modern engineering!

The reason it exists today is because it is based on technology from seven other bridges. The engineers stood on the shoulders of giants and learned from the engineers of the past. They adapted past things and made them better than they've ever been.

This can be related to your life. Many people tend to go through life trying to find their own way through things without learning from the people who have gone before them and who have created great lives for themselves and other people.

When I say great things, I mean what you consider great. It might be passing a certain test, running 5k or learning to walk again after an accident. We all have our own levels of what we think a great accomplishment is: if it's something we feel proud of, then that's good; but if it's something we feel proud of and it brings value to someone else's life, that's brilliant!

Robert F. Kennedy said it best when he said:

"Few people will have the greatness to bend history itself, but each of us can work to change a small portion of events. It is from numberless diverse acts of courage and belief that human history is shaped. Each time a man stands up for an ideal, or acts to improve the lot of others, or strikes out against injustice, he sends forth a tiny ripple of hope and crossing each other from a million different centres of energy. Those ripples build a current which can sweep down the mightiest of oppression and resistance."

CHAPTER 5

BUILDING MENTAL STRENGTH

"Our greatest glory is not in never falling, but in rising every time we fall."
– Confucius

If you have ever been over a suspension bridge like the Severn Bridge connecting Wales to England or the Golden Gate Bridge in California, you will notice there are huge steel cables supporting the bridge.

The cables look like one long thick cable going from end to end, but in fact they're made up of many different cables. On the Akashi-Kaikyo Bridge there are 36,830 strands of steel wire, each wire 112cm (44 inches). The big cables you can see weigh about 25,000 tones and contain enough wire to circle the Earth seven times... the overall length of the wire is 190,000 miles!

These steel wires combined hold up the bridge, and as I mentioned earlier, it can withstand huge earthquakes, tsunamis, and typhoons. It is without question one of the most advanced bridges in the world.

It is the same with building a great life and having happiness and confidence. These things are not formed in one event; they are formed in thousands of hours and experiences. Each positive experience we have is like a steel wire. When we are committed to being optimistic about things and we have another positive experience, it is like two steel wires combining and becoming stronger. It is the same with habits, the more success we have with new positive habits the more overall success we will have. Success breeds success!

In 1995, before the bridge was fully completed, the Great Hanshin earthquake (also known as the Kobe earthquake) hit and destroyed much of the area surrounding the Akashi-Kaikyo. The earthquake was devastating! It measured a whopping 7 on the Seismic Intensity Scale. Over 5,000 people were killed, over 36,000 people were injured, over 250,000 people were displaced, and it caused approximately $200 billion worth of damage.

So what happened to the Akashi-Kaikyo Bridge that was in the thick of it all? When structures all over the city were collapsing as easily as we can kick a sandcastle over, the Akashi-Kaikyo stood firm and survived. It was scarred from the devastating event, but it never collapsed, and to this day it still stands tall. When it comes to being tough, there are very few structures that are as tough as the Akashi-Kaikyo. The bridge was well thought out; thousands upon thousands of hours went into it being made, so planning is vital to success.

"It does not do to leave a live dragon out of your calculations, if you live near him."
– J. R. R. Tolkien (Author of 'Lord of the Rings')

It was made of special materials, and for that reason it didn't collapse when something devastating happened in the area.

It is like that in life: at some point in our life our mental world will be shaken up. Something will happen that can shake us at our very foundation, but if we are trained enough mentally and if we are strong enough, we will get through it.

So the more we feed our minds with positive material and thoughts, the stronger we will become and the better we will handle our own personal earthquakes, tsunamis, and typhoons in life.

The late, great motivational speaker and author Jim Rohn talked about the seasons of life. You will have springs, summers, autumns, and winters in life, that is inevitable. Jim Rohn is right; the hard times will come so prepare well but remember this:

"Iron doesn't become steel until it goes through the fire."

You can choose to get stronger or you can choose to break. Many people think that this choice is out of our hands, but we and we alone are responsible for how we decide to handle a situation.

Taking responsibility for our actions is thought of by many top achievers to be a sign of human maturity. It is what separates the men from the boys and the women from the girls. You and you alone are responsible for your mental attitude, even though you may not be responsible for what has happened to you. There are circumstances in life that happen to us which we simply have no control over, but we can control how we act when life kicks us in the balls.

Maybe there have been times in your life when you've felt secure in your job and then one day you get told you are no longer needed: "Bye bye!" You think, "Oh, great, now how am I going to pay for food, my rent, my mortgage, my car, the gas, the electric, the loans I have, etc?"

It is natural to think about all of those things and you may feel worried. But we have to remember that it is us that controls our thoughts regardless of the event. You can decide to interpret things so they will be to your advantage.

In 2013, I was mistakenly sectioned and locked up in a mental health ward. To cut a long story short, I was assessed on my mental health by four assessors and without them talking to any of my friends and family about me, they locked me up. I was unjustly shipped 52 miles away from my home and found myself staring at a wall in a mental health facility. Ironically, I felt incredibly strong mentally and had great mental health, so it was one of the most bizarre experiences of my life.

As I stood staring at the wall, I looked at this as a test. Rather than thinking, "Why me?" I thought, "Game on mother fuckers!"

I ended up breaking out of the facility, found myself on the run from the police, but in the end I claimed my freedom. I was later given a letter saying words to the effect of, "Mark shows no sign of mental health issues."

When I read the letter I thought, "No shit Sherlock, my friends and family could have told you guys that before you locked me up."

The point here is I decided to take control of the situation in my mind. I couldn't control what had happened, but I could control the thoughts I was having, and by controlling my own thoughts I came through winning in the end. You can do the same when life throws you a curve ball.

They say that out of every negative situation can come some benefit, and this was true in this case. I got to test how strong I was mentally, and I thought more clearly than probably any other time in my life. I had to get out of the situation. It also led to me completing another endurance challenge straight after I got out. And best of all, I've written a book about the experience.

CHAPTER 6

IT DOESN'T MATTER WHERE YOU START FROM – IT MATTERS WHERE YOU'RE GOING

"I would visualise things coming to me. It would just make me feel better. Visualisation works if you work hard. That's the thing. You can't just visualise and go eat a sandwich."

– Jim Carrey

I didn't do well in school, but school is really only the starting point of learning. Many people think like I did: if you don't do well in school then you're not going to do well in life.

This couldn't be further from the truth. If you've done well in school; then that can be a bonus that may lead you on to other things.

You could have two people, one brilliant academically but lacking drive and creativity, the other not as good academically but with lots of drive and creativity. The academic person could go on to achieve very little and the creative go-getter could go onto achieve great things. A perfect example of this is Richard Branson.

Generally, the person that succeeds is the guy or the girl who sets goals, is willing to learn, is focused and has lots of determination.

When I wanted to improve myself I read books, listened to cassette tapes, CDs and now YouTube and podcasts about how to achieve things. It is hardly rocket science; it may sound obvious to do this, but many people simply will not do it. They go to their 9-5 jobs and learn what they have to for their jobs, but when work is over they sit down in front of the TV and flick through the channels to see if they can find some form of entertainment to stop them from becoming bored.

There's nothing wrong with this, and it is not for me to judge what another person does with their life, but if you want to achieve on a high level, then you will need to invest your time in educating your mind rather than watching hours upon hours of TV every night.

One of the main reasons I've done so well in running is because I put the time into my training. I started out with very little fitness and after seeing me fail my 1.5 mile Army basic fitness test, you would have written me off as a decent runner. But I wasn't focused on my lack of fitness; I was focused on getting better. I wasn't focused on where I was; I was focused on where I was going. I had no idea that I would achieve so much, but I just kept on achieving one goal at a time. Every time I got to one level, I could see a bit further and think about going to the next level. The Chinese saying, "A journey of a thousand miles begins with a single step" is true.

In 2001, I decided to go for the 100k Treadmill World Record. There are many different ways to achieve a goal, and the way I decided to tackle this goal was to run 10k at a time.

When running a long distance like this you have to take in lots of water and, ideally, electrolytes. Electrolytes are mainly made up of sodium, potassium, magnesium, and calcium. They maintain the body's fluid balance and carry electrical energy to help the body function properly. Without these vital ingredients you can get cramps, weaker muscles, fatigue, dizziness, muscle spasms and a few other unpleasant things. Granted, if you're pushing your body you could get these things anyway, but taking on enough electrolytes will lessen the risk and keep your body working more efficiently. This all goes back to planning being vital to success.

Because I was talking in so much water and electrolyte drink, I would need to go for a pee every hour. This came in very handy for my 10k at a time goal. I would run 10k and then go to the loo (another top tip: make sure your pee is a fairly clear colour. If it's dark yellow, it means you're dehydrated, and you will lose a lot of performance). So I was focused only doing 10k runs at an easy pace, which was a strategy that worked well.

At the end of the run, I had comfortably broken the World Record. My legs were a bit tight, but I felt pretty good overall, and knew I could have run another marathon on top of the 100k. I had prepared well, and I was focused on where I was going.

With the Sahara Desert 130-miler over 6 days, I used a different strategy. We all set off in the morning and the only thought in my mind was, "I'm going to keep running all day until I get there." That strategy also worked.

With the 1600-mile run in the United States, I usually just ran until I hit a town or a certain campsite.

And with the Strava Distance Challenge, I just worked my way up until I came 1st on the leader board.

So there was no single strategy that worked: lots of strategies worked, but they all had one thing in common. I was focused on where I was going and not where I was.

It can be the same thing with what you take on in life. There may be more than one way to achieve your goal, but the main thing to do is... focus on where you're going, not where you are.

CHAPTER 7

CRITICS

"There is only one way to avoid criticism: Do nothing, Say nothing, Be nothing."

– Aristotle

If your goal is to make a better life for yourself and your family, I can guarantee you one thing: you will attract critics. The minute you announce that you are going to go for a big goal is the minute when you leave yourself open to criticism. It's just part of life.

The one thing you can take comfort from is that every single person who has achieved great things in their life has had critics. When Sam Walton started Walmart, you can bet your bottom dollar that people thought he was going to fail. Walmart later became the most successful supermarket chain in the world, with profits exceeding $14 billion a year and the largest business employer in the world, with more than 2.3 million employees. Even though Sam had the right to say, "I told you so", it wouldn't really matter, because whether you are rich or poor, fat or thin, good or bad, some people will still criticise you, it never ends.

I've even attracted the odd critic with my interviews. I remember someone on YouTube called me a Welsh twat, another person said I was no Jonathan Ross, and another person called me an absolute c**t!

If you want to achieve more out of life, then you will get more criticism. It's just the way things are, when you stick your head out of the crowd; expect to get a few tomatoes thrown at it.

Some of the most popular shows on TV today are things like American Idol, X-Factor and Britain/America's Got Talent. They do provide great entertainment; some people turn out to be amazing, and some are not so amazing. It's pretty easy to sit in the audience and laugh at some of the acts that come on, and I have to admit myself, that sometimes I think, "maybe it's time you tried something else, mate." So some criticism can be good.

There are basically two types of critic, those who have a genuine interest in helping you succeed in life and use constructive criticism and those who, no matter what you do, want to tear you down and see you fail. The challenging bit can be telling the difference between the two, because if you do not get this right it could mean the difference between success and failure.

Generally, people believe that friends that they have known for a long time will have their best interests at heart and will give them valuable support and advice. But before you take advice from any friends or family, you have to decide if they want to see you achieve your dreams. You must also look at the fruit on their tree to see if they have achieved what you want to achieve before you take advice from them. There are also those people who care about you who will try to suppress your dreams simply because they do not want you to be disappointed if you fail. I love my mum dearly and I know she loves me, but that does not mean I should take advice from her when it comes to living my life. If my mum had her way, I would have a 9-5 job for the next 30 years doing any job to get by, even if it was something that I didn't enjoy.

But settling for a job that I don't like has never been part of my game plan in life, and if you're in a job you don't like, get a new one. You may read that sentence and think "that's easier said than done, because I have bills to pay". There's a lot of truth in that, and I know I've taken jobs I didn't really love just to pay the bills and get by. If it's a temporary thing, that's fine, but if you're not happy in your job, you need to start looking for other possibilities. The danger for many people is they take a job temporarily and then they get stuck in that job for the next 5, 10 or even 20 years. Before they realised what's happened, they've wasted a massive chunk of their lives.

If you want to take the safe options in life, that's fine. You won't attract as many critics, but the downside to that is you will never achieve your potential and you could end up asking yourself the worst question in the word... "What if ?"

There are those people that will hate to see you succeed and be happy. For one reason or another they want to see you crash and burn. In fact, if something goes badly wrong in your life, there are people who would feel good about you failing. It is like the bully Nelson from The Simpsons TV show who points and says "HAHA" when something goes wrong.

We all have our Nelsons in our lives, but the key here is to not let them win. Yes, you will trip up and fail at certain things, and yes you will have people who doubt you, but if you listen to the critics, you may live to regret not being bold and just going for your dream.

Some people will tell you why you won't succeed, and other people will tell other people about how foolish you are to have your dream.

I recently came across this. The author is unknown, and it is apparently an experience that the Greek philosopher Socrates went through. Where it's from and how true it is I don't know, but I think there is something to be learned in this message.

In ancient Greece, Socrates was visited by an acquaintance. Eager to share some juicy gossip, the man asked if Socrates would like to hear the story he'd just heard about a friend of theirs. Socrates replied that before the man spoke, he needed to pass the "Triple-Filter" test.

The first filter, he explained, is Truth. "Have you made absolutely sure that what you are about to say is true?"

The man shook his head. "No, I actually just heard about it, and..." Socrates cut him off. "You don't know for certain that it is true, then. Is what you want to say something good or kind?"

Again, the man shook his head. "No! Actually, just the opposite. You see..."

Socrates lifted his hand to stop the man speaking. "So, you are not certain that what you want to say is true, and it isn't good or kind. One filter still remains, though, so you may yet still tell me. That is Usefulness or Necessity. Is this information useful or necessary to me?"

A little defeated, the man replied, "No, not really."

"Well, then," Socrates said, turning on his heel, "If what you want to say is neither true, nor good or kind, nor useful or necessary, please don't say anything at all."

You have probably come across this type of critic in your own life.

Life is too short to go around saying bad things about people and criticising other people all the time. If you focus on something negative, then the chances are you will become negative about life and people. Look for the good in people and avoid people who have only got bad things to say about everyone.

CHAPTER 8

YOU ARE LUCKY

"Be thankful for what you have; you'll end up having more. If you concentrate on what you don't have, you will never, ever have enough."

– Oprah Winfrey

Many people think to themselves, "I wish I was lucky; I wish something great would happen in my life," but the reality is there are always great things happening in your life. There are always miracles, but sometimes we take things for granted so we forget to see the little miracles. When I see my son Léon, I am in awe of the little miracle that is running around by my feet laughing and playing. When Léon calls me Daddy, it's just the best. When everything goes pear-shaped, I can take a step back and think about Léon and how lucky I am to have him in my life. But it is not just Léon that I am amazed by; there are many things to be grateful for. Good health has got to be the most important thing to be grateful for. Without health, life can be pretty miserable. You are living in a machine that is priceless. $100 billion could not create another person as unique as you, and sometimes we need to remember that.

When it comes to life expectancy, if you live in the Central African Republic, Sierra Leone, Zimbabwe or Zambia, your life expectancy is 45 to 46 years on average.

Compare this to countries like the UK, New Zealand, Australia, the US, Canada, France, and Japan which have an average life expectancy of 79 to 84 years. If you're from the western world, the chances are you're going to live a lot longer than if you live in certain other countries, so count your lucky stars.

When we look at the technology and the luxuries we have today, it is astounding to compare what we have now to what people had years ago. I was recently watching one of my favourite Leonardo DiCaprio movies, "The Great Gatsby".

There are people in the movie who are extremely wealthy, but what they had back then pales in comparison to what we have now. They may have had a bigger house, more land and a few more diamonds than most people would have today, but today we have so many items that people of 100 years ago could only dream about.

If you live in the developed world, then chances are you have access to most of the things available today. A hundred years ago there were no Samsung smartphones, no iPads, no computers, no microwaves, no DVD players, no Internet, no cheap flights abroad, no YouTube, no Google, no Facebook, no Twitter, no Skype, no digital cameras, no Amazon shopping, and no TVs.

We live better today than any king could have years ago: you don't need to go that far back to when they did not even have sewage systems in place. No toilets, no electricity, no gas, no cars, no roads, no planes, no helicopters, and no supermarkets with all of your food in one place.

Although all of these modern-day conveniences are great, the quality of your life is not governed by the things you have. The quality of your life is based on your emotional stability and the thoughts you think about yourself and what you think about your life.

If a billionaire thinks they are lacking something and focusing on what they have not got, then they may not be as happy as people think they would be. The trappings of success may look good from the outside, and it is certainly better to have some money than none, but if they are not happy, the person who has very little materially but who feels they have an abundance of good things has a far better mental state.

What we say to ourselves determines our actions, and our actions determine the outcome of our lives. Many people have no idea what they are doing when they are talking to themselves. It is so easy to put yourself down and talk negatively about yourself, but if you do this consistently, you will create a negative thought process that will lead to negative actions.

By believing that you are lucky, and you are a winner, you create a self-fulfilling prophecy. If you have low self-esteem like I once had, it may seem like you are lying to yourself, but the more you repeat this; the more you will start winning, and the more you start to win, the more of a winner you will become. You'll then get to a point where you just believe that you are a winner and things are going to work out for you. Life is not designed to let you win all the time, there will be good times and there will be hard times, but you can choose how you want to feel in the hard times.

Sometimes I hear people say negative words to themselves with a "Why me, poor old me?" attitude.

They feel sorry for themselves and have found comfort in playing the victim role. They moan and groan about anything and everything. They struggle to understand why life isn't going well for them and think the winners in life are just lucky. Yes, there is luck in life, but we make most of our luck ourselves. So rather than blame people all the time, we must take responsibility and take back control of our lives.

Yes, it's easier said than done, but it can be done. There are millions of people out there in the world who are living great lives. They have discovered the so-called Secret to Success, the secret to living a great live and being happy. If you want to be happy then look at all the things you have to be grateful for, enjoy the journey (not just the destination) and decide to be happy right now. Not tomorrow, not when you achieve your next goal, decide to be happy now.

In the chapter "Your Body Is A Miracle" you've read about how amazing you are and how powerful the human brain is. Remember that you are the person who is in charge of your brain, so point it in the direction you want to go and be happy now.

I recently watched the movie The Pianist for the first time and decided to watch Schindler's List again. Both films are an insight to what happened to certain groups of people during The Holocaust. Approximately 6 million people were mass-murdered, they were mainly Jewish but other persecuted groups including gays and Gypsies were beaten and ruthlessly executed.

While writing this book, I thought back to when I visited Auschwitz and Oscar Schindler's factory in Poland. I also thought about the time when I visited Anne Frank's house in Amsterdam in the Netherlands.

I thought about how lucky we are not to have gone through that. Sometimes we will hear on the news that there has been another mass shooting in America, or another terrorist attack somewhere. This can put some people into a state of fear, but it's nothing compared to the fear that we would have faced in a Nazi death camp. I have no doubt that there were many brave and tough people in the camps, but imagine how you would feel if you saw your loved one separated from you and you never saw them again.

You will see many people in the world of self-development claim to have made themselves successful solely through their own thoughts. While there is some truth in that, there is also luck involved. We have no control with what part of the world we were born in and no control what era it was in.

So always be grateful for what you have been given already. And even if you are facing challenging times right now, remember you are stronger than any challenge that will come your way!

CHAPTER 9

PERSPECTIVE

"There are no facts, only interpretations."
– Friedrich Nietzsche

Think you have always had it tough because of lack of money? Yes, it can be very difficult to get by without enough money, and to make many of our dreams come true we need money. But when we are feeling sorry for ourselves because we have not got enough, it may be worth putting things in perspective before we mentally beat ourselves up.

Let us take a look at things from a different perspective and see how many of us in the western world measure up to other countries in terms of having money.

According to dosomething.org:

- Nearly half of the world's population, that is more than 3 billion people live on less than $2.50 a day, and more than 1.3 billion people live in extreme poverty, that is, they live on less than $1.25 a day.

- 1 billion children worldwide are living in poverty and according to UNICEF 22,000 children die each day due to poverty.

- 805 million people worldwide do not have enough food to eat.

- 663 million people lack access to safe water and 1/3 of the global population live without access to a toilet, according to Matt Damon's charity water.org.

So when we look at things on a world scale, many of us are a lot better off than we think.

BEING IN THE TOP 1% OF EARNERS IN THE WORLD

Being a top earner on a global scale may not be as hard as you think if you live in a developed country.

At the time of writing there is a great website called www.globalrichlist.net where you can type in your annual net income and find out where you stand compared to the rest of the world.

If you earn:

- £10,000 a year, you are in the top 12.2%. Out of over 7 billion people on the planet that puts you comfortably in the top 730 million highest income earners on Earth.

- £15,000 a year, you are in the top 4.1%. Out of over 7 billion people on the planet that puts you comfortably in the top 250 million highest income earners on Earth.

- £20,000 a year, you are in the top 2%. Out of over 7 billion people on the planet that puts you comfortably in the top 115 million highest income earners on Earth.

- £25,500 a year, you are in the top 1%. Out of over 7 billion people on the planet, that puts you comfortably in the top 60 million highest income earners on Earth.

If you are like me and you live in a super-rich country, you will tend to see the odd glossy magazine with celebrities in. So just in case you are thinking what percentage they are in, let's take a look at a few other figures. If they (or you) earn:

- £100,000 a year, they will be in the top 0.07%. Out of over 7 billion people they will be in the top 4.1 million highest income earners in the world.

- £1 million net income a year, they will be in the top 0.008% and out of 7 billion people they will be in the top half a million highest income earners in the world.

- If you are David Beckham and earned £50.8 million in 2015 (according to express.co.uk) and are one of the highest earning retired athletes (according to Forbes.com), you are in the top 0.0001%. It's a tough life for some, but he does have a beautiful smile.

OK, that is money at an extreme level, but just because you are not earning David's type of money; it does not mean that you're not doing well financially.

If you are not working at the moment and you are over 25 and living in the UK and are claiming benefits (obviously it will vary for different countries and there are different types of benefits), you would be on roughly £73 a week which is £3,796 a year. You would be in the top 24% highest earners in the world without even working.

Yes, things are relative to what country you live in and food is probably cheaper in poorer countries, but if many of the people in the poorest countries (like the Central African Republic, the Democratic Republic of the Congo or Malawi) want to buy a Samsung Galaxy smartphone, an iPad, or a car, things can be a little more challenging, unless of course they become one of the higher income earners in their country.

I remember the time I lost my job; I woke up the next day and thought, "I cannot believe I am in this situation at this point in my life". Whatever happened to the large amounts of money I thought I would earn and had not made happen? I checked my bank balance, and I had £3.15. Even my son had more money than me, as a few years earlier I had put over £4,000 in his trust fund when I was earning a lot more than I did when I wrote the very first edition on this book. It was quite comical, really, but many people get so depressed about their financial situation it can lead them to a very dark place and some sadly even turn to suicide.

Even when it looks like you have lost a lot, there is still so much to be grateful for. On this particular day, I was up in the morning and putting my cereal in the bowl ready to have my breakfast. I thought to myself, "Hey, you still have a roof over your head, you are not going to go hungry, you still live in one of the greatest countries in the world and you are healthy enough to find work, even if it's to just get by for now". There is no need to compare yourself to the Beckham's of this world.

If you live in a developed country, you will still probably be in the top 25% income earners in the world, and if you are not in a developed country, then there are still lots of possibilities where you can change your circumstances and make a better life for yourself.

Everyone without exception who has made a dream a reality has suffered some sort of failure before they made that dream that reality. Here are a few examples of people who have failed and then turned things around to become successful.

One schoolboy was cut from his high school basketball team. His dream was to be a pro basketball player, so this was devastating to him. A setback like this would have put doubt in even the most confident person. He was so upset with being cut from the team, he went back to his house, locked himself in his room and cried. But he decided to pick himself back up and work harder than he had ever worked before. He not only went on to become a pro basketball player, he became a six-times NBA Champion, and became arguably the greatest basketball player of all time. That little boy's name was Michael Jordan.

"I've missed more than 9000 shots in my career. I've lost almost 300 games. 26 times I've been trusted to take the game-winning shot and missed. I've failed over and over and over again in my life. And that is why I succeed."
– Michael Jordan

One little boy was a late starter in life, and he couldn't speak until the age of 4. In school he did badly, and he failed his university exams. But being a slow starter and failing exams did not stop this boy. Later his work helped develop atomic energy, and he became the most influential physicist of the 20th century.

His name was Albert Einstein.

CHAPTER 10

STORIES – FROM FAILURE TO SUCCESS

"Try not to become a man of success, but rather try to become a man of value."
– Albert Einstein

One boy did not do well in school; his parents thought little of him, he spoke with a lisp and stuttered.

His name was Winston Churchill.

"If you're going through hell, keep going."
– Winston Churchill

One man was sacked from working for a local newspaper and was told he had no original ideas. He wanted to set up a park where children could go with their parents so the whole family could have fun. He also set up an animation studio that went bankrupt. Banks turned him away because they did not believe in him or his dream. Today, one of his parks employees around 62,000 people, and is 40 square miles in size; that's roughly the size of San Francisco. That man's name was Walt Disney.

"It's kind of fun to do the impossible."
– Walt Disney

One woman wrote a book and was rejected by 12 publishers. People did not believe in her or her book, but she kept on trying. She kept on asking people to publish her book. When a publisher eventually said they would publish her book, they also advised her to get a job because they believed she would not make much money. Her name is Jo Rowling AKA J. K. Rowling – author of Harry Potter.

"You might never fail on the scale I did. But it is impossible to live without failing at something, unless you live so cautiously that you might as well not have lived at all in which case, you failed by default."
– J. K. Rowling

One boy was cut from his team because the coaches thought he was too small, and he lacked the necessary skills to be a good football player. He later became the only player in history to win five FIFA Ballon d'Or's which was an award for the best football player in the world. His name is Lionel Messi.

"You have to fight to reach your dream. You have to sacrifice and work hard for it."
– Lionel Messi

One guy had a dream of making great movies, so he decided to apply to get into the University of California film school but was rejected twice. His name was Steven Spielberg.

"You shouldn't dream your film; you should make it."
– Steven Spielberg

One man failed in business, his fiancée died, and he lost 8 elections. His name was Abraham Lincoln.

"The best way to predict the future is to create it."
– Abraham Lincoln

One band was rejected by a recording studio who said they did not like their music, and they had no future in the music industry. The band ignored the criticism and carried on. Later they sold more singles and had more Number 1 albums than any other British act. According to the Recording Industry Association of America, they are the best-selling music artists in the US, and they hit the top spot with Billboard Magazine as the most successful of all time. They received 10 Grammy Awards, 15 Ivor Novello Awards, and an Academy Award. They are the most successful band of all time and have sold over 600 million records worldwide. Their names were Paul McCartney, Ringo Starr, George Harrison, and John Lennon... AKA The Beatles.

"I don't work at being ordinary."
– Paul McCartney

"Love one another."
– Ringo Starr

"I want to deal with what's in front of me now to the best of my abilities. In the end it is better to go for something and fail than to not go for it and live with regret."
– George Harrison

"Imagine."
– John Lennon

CHAPTER 11

GOING COMMANDO – THE WINNING MIND-SET

"Never give in. Never give in. Never, never, never, never."
– Winston Churchill

When you read self-development books, you will normally find that high achievers have a certain way of thinking. There are certain things they do; they have certain habits, and they think a certain way when it comes to how they'll achieve their goal.

It's never been so easy to access all of the latest information that will help you achieve your goals. When it comes to being a success at anything, it all boils down to hunger, how badly you want it and whether you're willing to go the extra mile to get what you want.

When I wanted to become a Commando and earn my Green Beret, the odds were massively against me. I wasn't the fittest, I wasn't the most intelligent intellectually, I wasn't the best at solving certain challenges and I wasn't the most confident.

What I was, though, was very, very hungry! I wanted that Green Beret as much if not more than any other person on my course, and as far as I was concerned, nothing and no one was going to stop me. When other people from my Junior Leader regiment had finished their work for the day, I was out training. When it was hot, I was out training. When it was cold, I was out training. When it was windy, I was out training ... And when it was hailing, ah, I'm being completely honest with this book. When it was hailing ... I took it as a sign to take a rest day and have a nice cup of hot chocolate.

But all jokes aside, you know when someone is really hungry for something because their effort shows up in their daily activity.

One of the big reasons many people fail to achieve their dreams is because they are afraid to take action because they fear failure. Ironically, by not taking action, they fail automatically. Many people do not even try to chase their dreams because they fear failing and looking like a fool.

Having failed the basic Army fitness test only 11 months before and having been voted fattest person in the troop, I looked a very unlikely, if not impossible candidate to pass this elite military course. Out of roughly 120 people in Junior Leaders Regiment, approximately 10 would attempt the course and only two, maybe three, would pass. The odds that I would pass the Commando Course and get into 29 Commando were slim, to say the least.

One of the reasons I wanted to be a Commando was because my cousin Martin Beckerleg was a Commando (serving with 40 Commando and Commando Logistic Regiment) and when I joined Junior Leaders Regiment Royal Artillery, I noticed there were certain staff in the regiment that were (at least that's what I thought) a cut above the rest. Although there were many good Sergeants in Junior Leaders, the ones that stood out the most were the ones that wore the Commando Green Beret and the maroon Para beret. I thought of these guys as special because they had passed tough courses that not anybody could do. They had passed courses that many people have failed, and that was the reason many people wanted to be in one of those regiments. Not everybody would try to get in these regiments, but given the choice, most of the junior soldiers I knew would love to be Commando or Para trained. One of the main reasons was because these guys were respected.

The main man on camp was a Scottish sergeant by the name of Eddie Reid. There were other people in the regiment that had a higher rank, more qualification badges, and more medals than Eddie, but the special thing about Eddie was he was the person in that regiment who had a Commando Green Beret along with a Commando Dagger badge on his upper left arm. To me this badge was worth 20 other qualification badges if not more, and no rank meant as much as having a Green Beret.

The other thing that I admired about Eddie was he was the fittest Sergeant. I would see Eddie out running and he was going at a much faster pace than I could run. He became a shining light for me as a boy soldier because he was different. In a sea of dark blue Army berets, Eddie's Army beret was green, which made him unique. I never thought about it at the time, but thinking back, Eddie must have also been an underdog when he went on the Commando Course. The reason for this is that Eddie's a fairly short guy, and lots of short people (even if they are super-fit) fail the course because many of them cannot carry the heavy backpacks.

Being strong in the Army can be a good thing, but nobody cares that much about it. In the Army, fitness is king, and the king of all fitness exercises is running. If you're a brilliant runner, you get the most respect. So even though I was rubbish at running, I always admired the fittest guys and dreamed about being one of these super-fit people one day.

I admired the fact that the Commandos were good all-round soldiers. They were good at both upper body and lower body fitness and they could operate in both extremes of hot and cold environments around the world.

When I used to go to the cookhouse (I would later call it 'the galley'), there was a photo on the wall of 29 Commando breaking the Military Marathon World Record.

For me that was it, I had to be a Commando, and I had to get into 29 Commando.

After having failing my basic 1.5-mile run, I'd passed 10 weeks later and got into the Army. By the end of the year I was the fastest in my troop on the 1.5-mile run and I was 6th in the battery out of around 120 people.

I went to the 29 Commando thinking I was pretty fit, but as I got to the top of one level, just like a football league, I was now at the bottom.

I failed the 29 Commando Beat Up twice. I passed the 3rd Beat Up by the skin of my teeth and passed the All Arms Commando Course on the 1st attempt, again, by the skin of my teeth.

The reason I got through it wasn't because I was brilliant, it was because I never gave in. If you want something badly enough, you've got to give it everything you've got and never, never, never, never give in.

CHAPTER 12

WHATEVER IT TAKES

"Nothing in this world can take the place of persistence. Talent will not; nothing is more common than unsuccessful men with talent. Genius will not; unrewarded genius is almost a proverb. Education will not; the world is full of educated derelicts. Persistence and determination alone are omnipotent."

– Calvin Coolidge

In 2014, people kept on telling me how good the Strava GPS app was and that I should download it to keep track of my running. After finishing a run one evening, I decided to finally download the app to see what all the fuss was about. I immediately noticed that it had different challenges you could do. The first one I saw was to see how fast you could run 10k, I had no interest in that. The second was to see how fast you could run a half marathon: again, no interest. Although I have respect for anyone who runs these distances, they weren't distances that appealed to me. I was starting to think that there would be no challenges on there that would be of any interest to me, but finally there it was... "how far could you run in a month". That was it; it was kind of like a Goldilocks and the Three Bears moment. The porridge is too cold; the porridge is too hot... ah, now this porridge is just right.

I was far from being in my best shape, but I had been doing some training. I was only around 75% fit at the time, but I thought I would go for it and see where I would come. There are many people out there who relentlessly train every day, and they always maintain a level of fitness that would be at least 90% of their top level. But that's not me, I train every week but if I'm not training towards something specific, I don't train at a very high level. As long as I'm lean and fairly fit, I'm happy with that.

I knew my fitness wasn't as good as it could be, but I set a goal to get into the top 5%. There were over 40,000 runners, so that meant getting into the top 2,000. I realistically thought the big dream for me would be to get in the top 1%, which would mean getting into the top 400.

The next day I set out on my run. Because I had work and other things to do in the day, I had to fit the running around everything else. After I had finished everything I had to do in the day, I set out on my run, I had no idea how many miles the other runners would do as this challenge was new to me. What I did know was that there would be a lot of people who wanted to do the best they could and rank as high as possible on the leader board, so there would be thousands of people who would want to beat me.

When it comes to running big distances, I have learned that it is better to start off slowly. When I did the Marathon Des Sables Sahara Desert run, I made the mistake of setting off too fast and started to pay for this lack of experience later in the run. From that day on, I have always preferred to start slowly with big distance runs.

You hear of people hitting the wall in the marathon at around the 18 mile point, but the wall doesn't exist if you have put in enough miles in training, you run the first 18 miles at a sensible pace and you've made sure that you've taken in enough carbohydrates and fluids on board.

Many people doing the marathon will follow a basic training plan which involves doing 3, 7 and 9 milers with the odd half marathon thrown in and a single 20-mile run thrown in before the marathon. This sort of programme is OK if you want to just get through the marathon, but for most of us, generally the more miles we put in the better the result we'll get. The elite marathon runners who get the best times are running anything from 100 to 140 miles a week. That many miles a week is something most of us can actually achieve when we put our minds to it. It may bring you personal best times and will get you to a level where you can beat the vast majority of the people who have entered the marathon, but beating the elite runners is a different story. For that you need the combination of the right training, nutrition, and genetics. If you are like me and weigh around 13.5 stone (189 lbs) it isn't likely you'll be beating a 9 stone elite marathon runner anytime soon. You may not have the greyhound-like speed, but there is a good chance you can do the distance.

When I set off on the first day of the Strava Distance Challenge it was December 1st, 2014. Although the weather can be good sometimes in West Wales, we generally don't have the best weather in December. For much of the run, it was more of a drizzle than rain, but I still got soaked. The weather I love to run in the most is in the heat, the hotter the better! When you are going for your dream, you don't always get perfect conditions, but often you have to make a start and keep going.

I don't remember exactly how many hours I was running for, but I do remember just plodding away and not worrying about the time or distance much. On the first day, I was just out there to get some decent miles in and see if I could get in the top 2,000. After I had been running for several hours, I decided to see where I was on the leader board. At the time of checking I hoped that I would be in the top 20,000 runners, but to my amazement, I was already in the top 400. I couldn't believe that I was already in the top 1%, and this motivated me to keep on going.

Sometimes you will have total belief that you will hit a certain goal and you will miss your goal. Other times you won't be so sure of hitting a goal, and something really cool and unexpected happens out of the blue.

Hitting the top 1% it was a lot easier than I expected, so my next goal was to get into the top 300, and if I was fantastically lucky, I may even finish in the top 150. I ran for another few hours and was thinking to myself, "I wonder if I'm in the top 250." When I synchronised to Strava I was shocked to see that I was now in the top 40. I was so pleased I took a screenshot, as I thought that might never climb that high on the leader board again. Here is another lesson for life.

When you put in slightly more effort than most people you put yourself into a much higher league.

Notice there I use the word "slightly." I had probably spent just a few hours more that day on my goal than many people, but it made a huge difference to the outcome in terms of what percentage group I had put myself into, and it can be the same with you with what you want to excel at.

However, putting yourself into the top 10% may take just a little more effort, but putting yourself into the very high levels means you usually have to put in a lot more effort. The closer you get to the top of the ladder in your chosen field, the more you will come across other people who are also very driven and who will also go the extra mile to be one of the best.

I kept on running again and I stopped to synchronise to Strava. It just kept getting better; I was now at 12th, out of over 40,000 runners. I could have been sensible here, finished at 12th and got some good rest in for the run the next day, but to hell with 12th, I now had to get into the top 10! I thought there will be other people out running so there was a possibility I could move down in the ranking, but the next time I synchronised it, it wasn't the case, as I was now number 6!

Again, I had surpassed my goal and now wanted to get into the top 5. Top 5 sounded good and I had to get into this prestigious group.

I ran until 2.30am, uploaded my miles and found out that I was now in 3rd place. I had gone through over 40,000 runners to 3rd, and this should have been enough for me. But I had come too far to come 3rd. It was cold and wet, and I was soaked to the skin, but I had to keep going.

While I was doing this run, my Uncle/Dad (who brought me up from a baby) Des was in hospital and in a bad way with a tracheotomy. He had smoked, drank (though not to excess, just a few a night) and eaten unhealthy for years and it had finally caught up with him. We didn't know if he would make it out alive.

During my time on the December Strava Challenge, I sometimes went up to the hospital to see him outside visiting hours. Although I wasn't extremely close to Des, I did love him and I always appreciated that he, along with my Aunt/Mum Diana, brought me and my brother Darren up after our biological mum Pat died.

When I started the challenge, I never thought I would do so well, but now I was close to the top of the leader board and I wanted to come 1st for Des.

I figured if I ran until 3.30am I would hit the top of the leader board, so I kept on going. After an hour of running, it was the moment of truth. I stopped and went to upload my miles to see if I was 1st. I was thinking this could be it; this could be my moment of glory! But as I looked at my phone, I stood there in disbelief as my GPS hadn't picked up the miles. I had been running for an hour for nothing, I couldn't believe it. I was still in 3rd place and it was now 3.30am. At that point I could have given up and settled for 3rd, but people who win in the game of life don't give in when they know they have more to give. There was no certainty that my GPS would work, but I went for it again and ran until 4.30am. I took my phone out of my pocket, synchronised the miles, and this time it worked. I was now 1st out of over 40,000 people.

I went into the hospital and told Des that I'd been doing a running challenge. I told him that I was trying to get to the top for him, but I was having a challenge with my GPS and a Scottish guy who was in 1st place, so it didn't look likely I was going to beat him. As he lay there looking at me with a tube down his throat I said, "But I carried on and managed to knock that Scottish bastard off the top."

He was clearly in a lot of pain, but he laughed, and I could see he was proud of me.

It was the last time I would see him laugh, as he passed away several weeks later.

After that first day, I thought all the top runners would put more miles in than I could do and I would be knocked out of the top 10, but it never happened. I consistently hit the top of the leader board for the next week until I picked up an injury and couldn't run any more.

I took the next 3 weeks off with the injury, and one day before the next challenge my injury was healed. I thought to myself, "I've had 3 weeks without any training, so it isn't realistic I'll come 1st again," as I always lose a lot of fitness when I have more than a few days off training. My goal this time was to come in the top 10. If I could come 8th, 9th, or 10th, I would be over the moon, but it never happened. I hit 1st place on the 1st day and consistently came 1st until my synchronisation broke down (the app stopped working for some reason) after a week of running. After 7 days, I was 23 miles ahead of my nearest rival in 2nd place and this time I was 1st out of 51,000 runners.

This is what I love about doing well in endurance: you have to earn it. There are certain things in this world that you can get by luck, like a slim physique, good looks, or money (if someone just gives it to you for nothing). But when it comes to achieving in the world of fitness, you have to graft for it. You've got to put the effort in, and you've got to push yourself both mentally and physically.

The main purpose of this story is to show you that:

1. You need a goal.

2. You need to put the effort in.

3. You need to persist when things are uncomfortable and when things go wrong.

CHAPTER 13

RUNNERS – THE BEST OF THE BEST

"The first race I ran, I fell."
– Usain Bolt

While I have done OK with running, there are people who have far surpassed my running achievements. Hang on a minute. If I'm writing a book to inspire people based on some of my achievements, should I really shout out about what great things others have achieved? After all, they may make my running achievements look tiny in comparison.

Having that thought process itself is a big achievement. Having the ability to let go of your ego to an extent is a good thing, because when you do that you see the bigger picture. You see that you are not the master of the universe and you are operating on a higher level of consciousness than maybe you were a few years ago.

Compared to the size of the universe, we as individuals are like a grain of sand on a beach.

So before we get all high and mighty because we have achieved one or two things, we need to also realise that whatever level we get to in this world, we are still tiny, tiny, fish in a very, very big pond.

Yes, even if you are a Prime Minister, King or President of a country or you are at the top of your game, it is still all small stuff in the grand scheme of things. That being said, each and every one of us is special and can make a positive difference in not only our own lives but also in the lives of other people.

When I started looking at people who have done ultra-running (running beyond a marathon) I decided to check out the main people in this sport. After a little bit of research, I came across a man who stood apart from everyone else. To put into perspective how good he is, he is the only runner to my knowledge that has been accused of cheating and the cheating accusation has eventually become a badge of honour. He was that good and that far ahead of everyone else, at his first official ultra-distance run, the officials thought it was simply impossible for a human to run that far and that fast in such a short time frame.

In 1983, a group of super-fit ultra-distance runners turned up for the first Spartathlon. Let us not get this confused with the Spartan Race. The Spartan races can be tough depending on how fast you want to run, and they're anything from 3 miles with obstacles to 26 miles with obstacles. These are great races, along with many other races that are popping up all over the world.

However, the Spartathlon is a completely different animal!

In order to even qualify for the Spartathlon you either have to:

- Run 100k (62 miles) in less than 10 hours 30 minutes; or

- Complete a 200km (120 miles) race in under 29 hours and 30 minutes.

The Spartathlon is a 246km (153 miles) beast of a race held annually in Greece, where the runners run from Athens to Sparta. Yes, that's right, if you have seen it, it's that place from the movie 300 where King Leonidas (played by Gerard Butler) shouts, "THIS IS SPARTA!" and kicks a rather rude person into a big pit.

I guess the moral of the story there is, don't go around threatening people and then stand in front of a very deep pit.

Anyway, this unknown runner rocks up to the Spartathlon and decides to take on a field of established international runners. Some the international runners were record-breakers, so it was assumed that the winner would come from this field of top runners. No one gave much thought to the newbie underdog who had showed up for the first time.

He ended up winning the event and was over two-and-a-half hours ahead of the person who came second. Everyone naturally thought this unknown guy had cut the course and cheated, so the next year he was watched like a hawk at every step by the race officials. The race goes over two mountain ranges with steep hills and rocky tracks. To the amazement of race officials and spectators, it took this man less than 7 hours to hit 100km. He got to the 100-mile point in less than 13 hours and ran the last 50 miles in under 9 hours.

He destroyed every top ultra-runner that took him on, and he broke world records left, right and centre.

In 1997, at the age of 41, he completed what is said by many to be the most phenomenal endurance feat in history. In the space of only 24 hours he ran 188 miles! That is the equivalent of 7 marathons back to back in one day. People sometimes talk about a long-distance runner being slow, but being slow is not a tag I would put on this man. When going for this 24-hour run, he ran the first 100k (62 miles) in 7:15. That's 31 miles in 3 hours 38 minutes. Many people would be happy to complete a 26.2 mile marathon in 3.38 never mind running 31 miles in that time and doing another 157 miles straight after.

In terms of the most phenomenal endurance feat in history, I would argue that there are two other superhuman feats that could challenge that. One man ran 1,000 kilometres (621 miles) in 5 days, 16 hours and 17 minutes. Throughout the 6-day race, he only slept for around 2 hours.

The other crazy feat was man ran a staggering 1,000 miles in in 10 days, 10 hours, 30 minutes, and 36 seconds... unbelievable! But that man is the same man I have just been writing about.

And that Underdog's name is Yiannis Kouros.

Yiannis Kouros holds World Records from 100 miles to 1,000 miles and went on to break over 154 world records. He became the greatest ultra-distance runner of all time.

"When other people get tired, they stop. I don't. I take over my body with my mind. I tell it that it's not tired, and it listens."
– Yiannis Kouros

When it comes to people who have achieved great things with running there is one other man in my humble opinion that blows everyone else away with succeeding on a grand scale for inspiring people. When I wrote the words "one man who blows everyone else away", I hesitated.

Not because I doubted his achievement, but because you could argue that he was still a boy when he achieved what he achieved. He was a young underdog who at the age of only

20 and in spite of tremendously challenging circumstances, got up and created something so outstanding it has never been beaten.

There are many runners that have covered more miles in a day, who have run much faster and who have run longer overall distances. What makes this young man's story so unique is he had cancer. He had one of his legs amputated and decided to run across Canada and raise $1 million, but things got a little bit bigger than that.

He was only 18 years old when he was diagnosed with bone cancer in his right knee. When he was in the hospital on the cancer ward he was affected by seeing children younger than him who had cancer. He said, "You just can't forget it, I couldn't anyway, I had to try and do something about it".

When I watched his story on YouTube, it reminded me of a quote which always stuck with me. The quote was from a deaf and blind lady who was an author, political activist, and lecturer, called Helen Keller. She said:

"I am only one, but still I am one. I cannot do everything, but still I can do something; I will not refuse to do something I can do."

This young man's thinking was in line with Helen Keller's. Even though we cannot sort all of the world's challenges out, we can all do a little bit to make the world a better place.

Before he set out to run across Canada, he trained for 14 months. His mother was concerned that it was too much for him and she wanted him to run a shorter distance, but his dream was bigger than that. He loved and respected his mother, but he knew he was capable of doing more, so he stuck with his dream. Even though some people may want to shrink your dream, ultimately you have to follow your heart and choose your own path.

On 12 April 1980, at the most easterly point of Canada, he began his run, which was called The Marathon of Hope. The goal was to run a marathon every day from coast to coast, which was over 5,000 miles. This would be a great achievement for anyone with two legs and in perfect health, never mind someone who had cancer and was running on a wooden prosthetic leg. He would get up at 4am and start running, no matter what weather he faced outside. For most of the run he was on his own: it was covered in some local papers, but not many people in Canada knew about it. Some local people would stop and put donations into buckets that his friend and brother held out while they followed behind him in a support vehicle. The road was lonely at times and the donations were very small. It looked very unlikely that he was going to raise $1 million, but he kept on going, he kept on putting the miles in.

Life can be a lot like that, we do the work, we put the effort in and sometimes no one seems to care. And even worse, there are many people who will tell you to give up. They will say or think things like:

- Give up, it is not worth it.

- What is the point in doing that?

- You cannot make a difference.
- You are dreaming.
- You have bitten off more than you can chew.

But high achievers always have these sorts of things said about them. The difference that makes them stand out as a high achiever is that they stick to their dream and keep going.

After two months of running, people started to believe in him and he was invited to a Canadian Football League game. When he entered the stadium, he was announced on the speaker system and all the football fans stood up, clapped, and cheered. This brought his thinking level even higher. Not satisfied with having a goal of raising $1 million, he decided that the goal should be to raise $1 for each Canadian, and back in the 1980s that was 24 million people. Would he raise $24 million? The odds were staggeringly against this underdog. These were the days of no smartphones, no Facebook, no Twitter, no YouTube, and no Internet, or at least not the Web as we know it today.

When he got to Toronto, thousands of people came out to support him, as he had inspired a nation. Things were going well, and he was going from strength to strength, he was putting in the miles, people from all over Canada were supporting him and the donations came flooding in.

He kept on running, but as he got to a place called Thunder Bay, he asked to be taken to hospital as he did not feel well. When the doctors examined him they found that he had big tumours on both sides of his lungs. Several days after that, he was taken to hospital in Vancouver and a fundraising telethon was organised. He had raised over $2 million and the telethon raised over $10 million more. He later told his mother that his biggest regret was that he did not have a single dollar to buy his family a Christmas present, even though he had raised millions for cancer.

He wrote in his journal, "If I die, at least I'll die happy doing what I wanted to do in life."

On 28 June 1981, he sadly passed away. He ran 3,339 miles (5,373 kilometres) across Canada and on the back of that annual runs were launched. They are now in countries all over the world and have raised over $650 million.

They are the world's largest one-day fundraiser for cancer research.

In the end, the young Canadian underdog inspired people all over the world. He created something spectacular. And he won! This amazing man's name was Terry Fox.

"I want to try the impossible to show that it could be done."
– Terry Fox

CHAPTER 14

WINNERS AND LOSERS

"There is nothing noble in being superior to your fellow man; true nobility is being superior to your former self."
– Ernest Hemingway

If you genuinely want to change your life, then you must change the things you are doing on a day-to-day basis.

Many people want change in their lives but simply do not change anything they are doing to make things better. They sit around and wish for a lucky break. Generally, the so-called lucky break will come after a series of failures, which involve trying something out. If you sincerely want to change things, then you must be willing to change.

It is very easy to look for excuses not to change. Many of us look at people like pop stars or movie stars and say things like, "It is easy for them to stay in shape; they can afford personal trainers". Of course they can afford personal trainers but you, too, can get trained for either a small amount of money or no money.

There may be something you can offer the trainer in return: a product or service that you are expert in. I had one client who was good at certain areas of marketing, so I said, "Rather than you pay me, how about you help me with marketing, and I'll train you?" We swapped an hour of my time for an hour of his time; it was like the old bartering system, and it worked well.

Or you can find a friend that is willing to do some training with you. At first you may struggle to find one of your friends who does fitness training. It's easy to rationalise it and say, "I can't find anyone to train with" and give up. You have to move into a different group of people, I am not saying you have to leave all your friends and never communicate with them, I am saying to be a success at something you need to find someone who is already successful at what you want to succeed in. I cannot emphasise this point enough.

Being around that person will motivate you to achieve things you have never achieved before.

I recently saw a trainer on YouTube who was raising his voice and calling people a fucking loser if they had not achieved certain things with their lives. Some people respond to this sort of talk well, and for others it makes them feel like crap. But no one on this Earth is a loser: we all have an important role to play in this world, and everyone's actions will send out a ripple in the pond of life. You can send out positive, loving, encouraging messages or negative, criticising, hateful messages. What sort of ripple we send out is up to us. Just remember that the boomerang you send out will be in the boomerang you get back. Of course, you can be nicest, happiest, friendliest, most loving person in the world and life can still bring you to your knees. We will all go through tough times, but the nicer and more giving we are, the more likely it is that life will bring us the same in return.

Sometimes people say negative things because the other person may have hurt them in some way, but if you are going around calling people a loser because you have achieved more than them, maybe you need to practise some humility. We all start from somewhere and we all have our own personal journeys. If you are making progress in an important area of your life, then you are a winner, and if you have hit a roadblock and are not progressing, then maybe it is time to take a step back and assess the situation. It could be you need to take a different approach or it maybe you just need to persist more.

If you think "I am a winner and you are a loser," maybe it's time to read some books like the "Tao de Ching" or read some Jesus and Buddha quotes. How many times did you hear or read about people like Jesus, Buddha and other great people saying, "You're a loser?"

As I am writing this I am literally laughing, because it is crazy to think that was the sort of thing they were teaching.

The truth is, you and I are no better than someone else as a human being just because we may have come first in a high-level fitness competition or have more money or have a high level of status because of what we have achieved. There is nothing wrong with having these things, and yes, it is probably better to be super-fit and healthy than to not, and it is probably better to have a lot of money in your pocket than not. But just because someone has a big belly or a low-paid job, it does not make them a loser. You will be able to learn something from each individual on this planet. You may not agree with them, but you can always learn something.

CHAPTER 15

PERCEPTION

"No problem can be solved from the same level of consciousness that created it."

– Albert Einstein

One of the greatest movies ever made that covers perception has to be The Matrix. Just in case you haven't seen it, the character Neo is in his little bubble world and is told to believe certain things by the men in suits. I would love to go deeper into this film, but for the purpose of this book I won't. To cut a long story short, Neo unplugs from the system and reaches his full potential.

The system you are plugged into will affect your life, for better or for worse.

Many times, people watch the news and are fearful for their lives because of some danger out there in the world. Sometimes the news can be of great use to us. An example of this would be news of a hurricane that is about to hit where we live. With this sort of warning, we can batten down the hatches or head out of town until the storm has passed. But all too often negative things are reported in the news which builds a climate of fear, terrorist attacks being one of them.

I remember taking to a guy who refused to go to London because he believed that he may get killed in a terrorist attack. He had watched so much negative media it got to the stage where it controlled his life.

Of course it's possible he could get killed, but let's look at some facts to see what the chances are

According to Global Research:

- You are 271 times more likely to die in a workplace accident

- You are 1,904 times more likely to die in a car accident
- You are 33,842 times more likely to die from cancer
- You are 35,079 times more likely to die from heart disease
- You are more likely to die from being struck by lightning than being killed in a terrorist attack.

Since 9/11 about 24 people have died from terrorism in the United States: at the same time more than 100,000 people have been killed in gun-related crime and over 400,000 people have been killed in motor vehicle accidents.

Like many people in the UK, I don't have a religion, however I do believe in a higher power. Whether you have a religion or not doesn't make a difference to me, as I see people as people. But I thought it would be interesting to look at some facts about the religion that is arguably the most vilified religion in the western world.

According to the Huffington Post, the FBI conducted a survey and found that 94% of terrorist attacks in the United States have been by non-Muslims. This means that an American terrorist suspect is over 9 times more likely to be a non-Muslim than a Muslim. In 2010–2015, there were over one thousand terrorist attacks in Europe: what percentage of these attacks were by Muslims? If you're living in the UK or another country that has media and government who are a little on the anti-Muslim side, then the chances are you would believe that at least 80% of those 1,000 + attacks are by Muslims. However the reality is quite different, it's less than

2%. A study was carried out by the University of North Carolina, which showed that fewer than 0.0002% of Americans killed since 9/11 were killed by Muslims.

In 'The Week', it has been reported that there are 1.6 billion Muslims and close to 1.6 billion Muslims have not committed an act of terror.

WHAT IS A TERRORIST?

According to the FBI official website, there is no single, universally accepted definition of terrorism. Terrorism is defined in the Code of Federal Regulations as "the unlawful use of force and violence against persons or property to intimidate or coerce a government, the civilian population, or any segment thereof, in furtherance of political or social objectives".

If you ask many people in the UK if the British are terrorists, of course they will say no. But if we were to look at the past activities of the British within the definition given earlier, then Great Britain doesn't come out squeaky clean here. The British Empire was the biggest empire by land mass in history, and it didn't become that way by asking another country if it could simply take over their country.

I was watching a James Bond movie once where 007 had a meeting with a guy. As they were talking, the man said, "One man's terrorist is another man's freedom fighter."

This made me think about how everything boils down to perception. It's about the environment you're in and what you choose to believe. Many people in Northern Ireland believed the IRA were freedom fighters wanting to get rid of oppressive British rule, but to most people in Great Britain the IRA were terrorists who would all ruthlessly murder innocent people and British soldiers.

So, a lot of conditioning is done from governments and media and many people will believe them. It's brainwashing on a national or even a global scale. It's mainly to do with the people being in charge having more of an influence than the average person. Many of these leaders are influential, they have a belief about something, (even though they could change that belief in the future), and they will push their belief onto other people, even if the facts are wrong. An obvious example of this is the Iraq war.

Don't get me wrong here: I'm not having a political rant or pointing the finger. It is not my place to judge and of course I love being British, but the purpose here is simply to show how people are conditioned and everything is down to perception.

Most people will not let go of certain conditioning, as this can lead to admitting that they were wrong about something, and none of us want to be wrong. None of us want our ego damaged and have to admit that we are not as clever as we thought we were. With this part of the book, you may need to keep an open mind. There are even some people who have been conditioned so strongly that they may reject what is said here, but there is nothing wrong with that.

Part of having a great state of mental health is having the

ability to flow with things, rather than get all bent out of shape and angry. It's far better to be like water, where you can flow around things and gradually wear the situation away over time. But there are also times when you have to stand firm like a rock in certain situations.

There are many ways to solve challenges, and in the end only you can decide how to handle those challenges. Every single human being on this planet is a product of what they have fed their minds or what they have been fed by different sources. We may all think that we are too clever to be led by other people, but we are all influenced by certain things.

Here is a question you could ask yourself: "Have you ever had a belief about something that you later found out wasn't true?" I know I have.

This was highlighted to me while writing this book. Léon's tooth was wobbling, and it looked like he was about to lose his first tooth. While on the phone one day to his mum, she mentioned that this would be the first tooth he would lose. As it was my weekend with him, there needed to be a plan in place where if his tooth came out, I would have to put a £2 coin under his pillow from the tooth fairy. I didn't have to do it, but this wasn't a big deal and so I went along with it.

Was a tooth fairy going to leave a £2 coin under Léon's pillow? As adults we all know the answer to that (at least I hope we all do), but children all over the world are convinced that a tooth fairy exists, and I know I did at one time, like many of us.

How many of us believed that Santa Claus was real at one point in our lives? If you are from many of the western world countries and are a certain religion, then you will probably say you did believe. If you're from a certain isolated tribe deep in the Amazon jungle, then you wouldn't have believed in the Tooth Fairly or Father Christmas. If they knew that you used to believe that an elderly overweight man would climb down your chimney on 25 December every year, while delivering over a billion toys worldwide by means of flying reindeer, I'm sure many of them would think that you've lost the plot.

There are few, if any tribes that haven't been discovered, but I'm sure that if you walked into their tribe with a phone, and a microwave oven (because that's the kind of thing you'd always carry in the jungle) there would be a look of shock on their face. Saying that, when I was on jungle warfare training, I think I would have had a look of shock on my face if someone walked into our camp carrying a microwave oven. You'd be like, "What the fuck?!"

Does that mean you are smarter than them because you know more about technology? No. Does it make them smarter than you for not being fooled into believing in Father Christmas? No. It just means that you have been exposed to different things.

Of course there are people that will say, "Yes, but I was only a child back then," but people can be fooled at any stage of their lives.

Several years ago, I did a 6 month United Nations peacekeeping tour with 29 Commando. One day a riot broke out. At one point I saw a Greek man launch a stone towards the Turks, but the stone hit another Greek man on the back of the head. The man who was hit held his head as the blood poured out of it. Later that evening, I was watching TV. I saw the same incident that I'd witnessed that day being covered on TV. I saw a Turk throw a stone; next I saw the same Greek man that I had seen before holding his head with the blood pouring out of it. I immediately thought that it just didn't happen that way. The Greek man hit the Greek man, but the media edited it to make people believe what the media wanted them to believe. This was the first time I saw how the authorities control how people think and how media can shift people's perceptions.

So before you decide to take on a belief, decide if that belief will help you and, as Einstein said, "the important thing is not to stop questioning."

CHAPTER 16

THINK FOR YOURSELF

"Thinking is the hardest work there is, which is probably the reason why so few engage in it."
– Henry Ford

If you want to achieve big things in life, then you can't be like the majority of people. There is nothing wrong with being average, and if you achieve more than the average person it doesn't necessarily make you a better person. What it can do, though, is give you a sense of pride, and by achieving your goals you might inspire other people, too.

I was talking to my friend Jack Woods one day about how people generally follow the crowd and feel comfortable with that. He referred to most people as "sheeple". At the time I hadn't heard of that expression, but I immediately knew what it meant. Many people follow each other like sheep and have a hard time thinking for themselves. It made me laugh, but I did think it was a good expression.

I was coming over a toll bridge one day and noticed that there were four cars in a queue in one of the lanes. The lane had a green light above the toll which meant it was one of the lanes you could use to get through the toll. I noticed that there was a green light above the lane next to it, but no one was using it. Although people could use the lane, no one was. The reason... they were following the crowd. I passed all the cars that were lined up and went straight to the front of the empty lane, paid my toll, and went through the barrier.

On another occasion, I was out running one morning and was approaching a set of traffic lights. I noticed as I was approaching there was a man standing there waiting for the traffic lights to change to green so he could walk across the road. I noticed that there was no danger from getting hit by a car, so I simply ran across the road.

Waiting for the traffic lights to change to green is often good practice because of safety issues, but there are times when you have to break the rules, go against the norm, and make a decision for yourself. Many people live in fear and never achieve their dreams because they are afraid to think for themselves. They are afraid that they'll get told off by the authorities or that other people will criticise them. If you want to achieve big things, you've got to take chances and take risks. I'm not saying you should get a new career as a cat burglar, but I am saying if you want to live an exciting life you need to have the courage to go after your dreams. On your journey you will stumble, you will fall, you will get knocked back and you will fail at certain points, but you can pick yourself back up and drive through to success!

A similar thing happened when I was in London, walking through the bus station to catch my bus back to Pembrokeshire. A fleet of buses were heading out of the station onto the road. At one point, several of the buses couldn't get out of the station and had to wait for the traffic on the road to clear. One bus stopped directly in front of where I wanted to go so we all stopped and waited for the bus to move out of our way. After about five seconds, I realised that no one knew when the bus would get out of the station, so I decided to walk around the back of the bus and carry on towards my destination.

And guess what happened when I walked around the bus? A load of other people followed me.

These are very simple stories that can happen in everyday life, but the simple point is that many times we need to be the one that makes the move; we need to be the one that takes that first step. Just because an obstacle has been put in our way, it doesn't mean that it's the end of the road for us when it comes to reaching our goals.

At some point in your life there will be a time where you have no experience with what you want to achieve, but if your dream is big enough, you will find a way.

Sometimes the traffic lights are on red, telling you that now is not the time, but sometimes you can't wait for all the signs to say "Go!"

Sometimes you have to give yourself that green light and make the move.

CHAPTER 17

NOT EVERYONE WILL UNDERSTAND YOUR IDEA

"All our dreams can come true if we have the courage to pursue them."

– Walt Disney

You may have a vision for something that is totally original and outrageous, and you're sure it will work. The more original and outrageous your idea is, the harder it can be to convince people it's a good idea.

I consider myself to be a pretty open-minded person, but if someone came up to me in 1998 and said they were going to create a cartoon with the storyline of a pants-wearing sponge living in an underwater city called Bikini Bottom and said it'd be a huge hit one day, I would have thought this person was a little crazy. When I say crazy, I mean it in a good way, because if someone said that to me, it would definitely bring a smile to my face, but at the same time, I would wish them all the best with it.

Just because I can't see someone's vision, it doesn't mean that person's vision will never materialise. We all have our opinions on things, but as wise as we think we are, the truth is, our knowledge is limited.

I was sitting down with Léon one day when Sponge Bob Square Pants came on the TV. After watching a bit of it I was in disbelief at how successful the cartoon has become, which lead me to do some research on how it started and exactly how successful it now is.

Sponge Bob Square Pants was created by a marine biologist called Stephen Hillenburg, and like Walt Disney, Hillenburg liked to draw.

Many people reading this book may already know that the Sponge Bob character is very energetic and optimistic, which are two keys to reaching your goals, even if you aren't a sponge.

Before Hillenburg created Sponge Bob, he created another animation called The Intertidal Zone, which taught students about the life of animals in tide pools. He tried to get his comic published but was turned down by everyone he sent the comic to.

He then made an animation film called Wormholes, which was about the theory of relativity, and he met Joe Murray, who was the creator of a popular Nickelodeon animated series. Murray offered Hillenburg a job, Hillenburg got his foot in the door with Nickelodeon, created a character out of one of the strangest sea creatures, and the rest is history.

Stephen Hillenburg's Sponge Bob Square Pants went on to win 12 Kids' Choice Awards, 8 Golden Reel Awards, 6 Annie Awards, 2 Emmy Awards and 2 BAFTA Awards. It is the most distributed property of MTV and the highest-rated series in Nickelodeon's history, and the media franchise has generated a staggering $8 billion. Stephen Hillenburg now does what he loves doing and has pocketed over $90 million in the process.

Even though I don't get the whole Sponge Bob thing, I love the story of how it was made and there is no denying that Stephen Hillenburg and his team have gone on to create something very special that many children (and some adults) love.

Here are some of the key principles that Stephen Hillenburg used to succeed. They are also the keys to success in running, sports, public speaking, business, the arts, or anything else:

1. Have a vision.

2. Do something you are passionate about.

3. Start small and build up to greater things.

4. Create a product or brand.

5. Get your foot in the door with the right people and organisations.

6. Learn from the people who have done the type of thing that you want to do.

7. Never give in, even if you get rejected by lots of people.

CHAPTER 18

SEIZING THE DAY

"Learn from yesterday, live for today, hope for tomorrow."
– Albert Einstein

Many people have this thing where they want to save all their money for a rainy day. There is nothing wrong with that, but what is crazy is working all the time and never having any fun time. By all means work hard, but if you don't reward yourself along the way, then what's it all for? A few years ago I was a support worker where I would take people out who had certain challenges (epilepsy, brain injury, learning difficulties, etc.). I had been taking a gentleman in his early 50s who was challenged with epilepsy for several years, and I was on my way to his house to take him out for a few hours. As always, I arrived at his dad's house where he lived, knocked on the door and waited for the door to be opened. After a few minutes, his dad opened the door. I went into the usual routine and asked whether my client (his son) was ready to go out for a few hours, to which his dad replied, "He's not here". There was nothing unusual about this, as my client often went for a walk on his own, and I usually had to go and find him.

"When will he be back?" I asked. His dad said, "He's gone".

"Gone where?" The answer from his dad took me aback, as it wasn't something I expected to hear: "He's dead". Complete silence. It was like one of those scenes you see on TV where tumbleweed blows past you in the wind.

It turned out that he had died in the night. I couldn't help feeling for his poor dad who had only just lost his wife a year or two before and now his son was gone.

One of the things that I thought about was how my client loved Elvis and how he had always dreamed about going to

Graceland for a once-in-a-lifetime trip. He had the money in his bank account to make the trip a reality and I encouraged him to take the trip, but sadly he never did. His dream of seeing the King of Rock-and-Roll's house died with him. It was something I'll never forget, and it made me think that we should seize the day when we can, because we never know what's around the corner.

CHAPTER 19

TAKING OPPORTUNITIES

"When one door closes another door opens; but we so often look so long and so regretfully upon the closed door, that we do not see the ones which open for us."

– Alexander Graham Bell

In 2015, I was asked to do security at a military camp. The question I was asked was, "Would you like to do some security work at a military camp?" My answer was, "No, not really." But after I'd said that, I felt that I needed to know where the camp was and asked. The answer that came back was, "It's in a place called Trecwn." This immediately got my interest up. In Pembrokeshire, Trecwn is well-known to some people as a kind of an Area 51 place. It has always been out of bounds to the public as far as I was aware, and all I knew about it was that it was used as a military base in World War 2 where it stored ammunition, but I wasn't even sure of that. I was 90% convinced that I wanted to go there just to have a look around, but I asked a second question: "What's happening there?" The answer came back, "I'm not supposed to say anything about it, but some ex-Special Forces guys are doing some sort of TV show there. That was it... I was sold! I didn't even care about being paid, I just wanted to get into this mysterious place and meet the ex SF lads.

I ended up doing the security on the camp for the TV show that was about Special Forces Selection (it was later released on Channel 4 as SAS Who Dares Wins).

I met some of the lads who were ex-Special Forces and we had a chat about what we were doing now and in the future.

It was great talking to the SBS (Special Boat Service) guys who had done the same sort of course as me in the forces. As we chatted, I told Ollie and Foxy that I had a lot of respect for what they'd achieved. I remember saying, "Fair play, guys, you took it to the next level with going for the SBS after the Commando Course."

They were gracious and humble about the compliment, and I admired that about them. Do you have to be gracious and humble to be successful? You only have to look at Muhammad Ali or Donald Trump to know the answer to that question. So you can be successful by having a different personality to other successful people.

Although I never had an interest in going into the SAS or SBS, I've always had lots of respect for them for passing such a tough course. Out of every 100 people that go for the course, only 10% (or fewer) make the grade.

I showed them some of the things I'd done since leaving the forces and as I was walking off, Ollie turned to me and said, "Seriously, mate, that's really impressive, what you've achieved!"

People that know me well know that I don't really crave praise, but I have to say that Ollie's comment really made me stop and think. I have a lot of respect for what Ollie's achieved by passing the Commando Course, SAS Selection and the SBS Course, and I was extremely grateful that someone from a unit that I respected so much would say something so nice to me. I can honestly say I had a "moment."

It made me think back to when I had little confidence and was bullied, and when I thought I was destined to achieve very little in life.

Sometimes it's difficult to believe you will achieve big things, I certainly would never have believed that I would have achieved the things I have done. But it all starts with having a goal, taking action, and grabbing opportunities with both hands.

If you're overweight and you want to get fitter and slimmer, great. The chances are you have two legs, so you have a great opportunity to go for a run or go out cycling.

If you want to build a better body for yourself, great. The chances are you've got a set of arms, so you have a great opportunity to do some push-ups or pull-ups or lift some weights and change yourself.

I interviewed former Royal Marines Mark Ormrod and Joe Townsend, who lost limbs whilst serving in Afghanistan. Both Mark and Joe are doing great things in the world of fitness. Yes, they both lost their legs (Mark also lost an arm), but they decided that there was still an opportunity for them to achieve great things. They took their lives to the next level and inspire people from all over the world.

CHAPTER 20

BEING A DIAMOND

"A diamond starts out rough and unpolished. But with enough pressure and in the right hands, it becomes tough and shines, and so can you."

– Mark Llewhellin

There are very few things that will be as important to you as building mental toughness. This is something that I talk about several times throughout this book, simply because it is one of the most important things you can do in life. You can be born into a life with great parents, you can have great genetics, a great physique, lots of money, great looks and every advantage that can be given to you, but if you do not develop mental toughness, life will chew you up and spit you out! The tougher you are mentally, the easier you will find things when life sends its inevitable challenges your way.

- A diamond is made from carbon, the same element that makes graphite and coal.

- Diamond is the hardest material known to man because of the way it has bonded together.

- Both graphite and diamond are made from carbon, but their structures are very different.

It is the same with people: we are all made from the same stuff (carbon also being one of the elements), but we are not all the same when it comes to how much we achieve and how strong we are mentally. People who achieve highly in life bond certain habits and certain principles together that leads to success.

The difference between graphite and diamond is very subtle, but there is a difference. With the habits we use in our daily life, that tiny difference makes a world of difference in the end. When we see people walking down the street, they all pretty much look the same on the outside. Yes, of course there are differences, but most of us have ears, mouths, noses, eyes, arms, and legs, etc. But what we cannot see is what's going on internally in our brains and how things are bonded together.

Experts believe that diamonds are created at roughly 100 miles below the Earth's surface and can take millions or billions of years to form. Like the diamond, it takes time for us to mature and develop into something brilliant. You don't get super-fit by having the odd run. You become super-fit from years of practice. And it's the same with any craft; it takes time, patience and relentless persistence to shine.

Diamonds are formed deep in the Earth's mantle, which is the layer between the Earth's crust and the extremely hot core. Down there it changes the molecular structure of carbon by crushing the atoms together and forcing them into a new structure, making it extremely tough. Under extreme pressure and temperatures carbon becomes diamond, and the diamond gets to the surface through rare, violent volcanic eruptions, which are then blasted to the surface in a host rock called kimberlite.

Like the diamond deep in the Earth, we will also go through challenging times and face extreme pressures and dark moments when we may feel there is no way out.

As the kimberlite transports the diamond, we can also use transporters to help us through to the surface and the light.

These transporters can come in several different forms. They can come in the form of reading self-development books, listening to inspirational people or through friends and family helping us. No matter how tough you are, there will be times when you need outside support. As the old saying goes, no man is an island.

Diamonds occur naturally in the Earth, but getting the diamond out of the Earth is very tough. For every 1 carat of diamond you have to move approximately 200 tons of rock.

Having a high level of mental toughness and success requires digging deep, and the higher you go in life, the deeper you will have to dig.

Characters are formed through challenging circumstances. Every one of us will face challenges in life whether it be moral, financial, physical, or mental. Challenges are just a part of life that we have to accept, and we can either rise to the challenge or crumble and give up. The choice is ours!

Yes, the choice really is yours; you will be the one that decides how you are going to react to a certain situation. You can think your situation is hopeless and you will never get out of it, or you can decide that you are too strong for anything to destroy you mentally. Of course, this is easier said than done but, you are stronger than any situation that will ever get thrown at you.

So if you're looking to take your life to the next level, be prepared to go through some dark times and get crushed and put under extreme pressure. And by following many of the principles in this book, you will come out like a diamond, tough and shining for all to see.

"When you are inspired by some great purpose, some extraordinary project, all your thoughts break their bonds: Your mind transcends limitations, your consciousness expands in every direction, and you find yourself in a new, great and wonderful world. Dormant forces, faculties and talents become alive, and you discover yourself to be a greater person by far than you ever dreamed yourself to be."

– Patañjali

DELUSIONS OF GRANDEUR

How To Become More Than You Ever Dreamed Possible

MARK LLEWHELLIN

INTRODUCTION

Delusion definition:

1. A false belief or opinion about yourself or your situation.
2. The act of believing or making yourself believe something that is not true.

– Oxford Dictionary

Grandeur definition:

1. The quality of being great and impressive in appearance.

– Oxford Dictionary

Delusions of grandeur definition:

The belief that you are more important or powerful than you really are.
– Cambridge Dictionary

Okay, so here we go with the first question, why another personal development book?

The reality is, there can never only be one book on personal development that is relevant to everyone as we all interpret things differently.

We all like different stories, we all have different needs, we are all unique and there aren't just one or two stories to tell – there are hundreds if not thousands, of inspiring stories to tell.

It's the same with any genre, whether it's romance, thriller, or action and adventure. How many times have we seen an underdog go out in a movie against impossible odds, win the battle and get the girl (or guy) and become a big success?

It's a common story, but it's a story that we all love, and each story is told differently.

Writing about personal development is also what I love to write about because I've seen the changes books like this have made in peoples lives as well as my own.

It seems like a bold subtitle, "How To Become The Person You Dream Of Becoming," but I can confidently put that subtitle because I am now the person I always dreamed of being. And I know that if I can become the person I dreamed of becoming, achieve the things I once dreamed about and live a life that was once an impossibility for me, then anyone else can do the same.

All I've done is put together the research to get the very best information out there from people who have achieved brilliant things in their lives.

Yes, there are things that you and I can learn from our own experiences, but much of what we learn is from other people.

I'm hoping that this book will give you a shortcut to achieving your own goals so you can avoid many of the mistakes that I made.

So how did this book come about?

A few years ago, a friend messaged me and said she was upset because someone had messaged her and said a few unkind things about me.

The person that messaged my friend was one of my old school friends.

As often happens in life, you leave school and you drift away from many of your friends, at least that was the case before the days of Facebook, and it was certainly the case with me and him.

Now after over 20 years of almost no contact with him, he turns up out of the blue and decides he isn't happy with what I'm doing with my life.

He could see that I have big dreams and goals but instead of saying things like, "go for it," or "I hope Mark makes it happen," or "I sincerely wish Mark all the luck in the world," he thought it would be better to message my friend (who he didn't even know) and tell her that I have delusions of grandeur.

My friend who told me about this situation was terribly upset about this guy's actions and couldn't work out why someone was ripping into me like this.

Not only this, I noticed every now and again he was posting on my Facebook comments section things that weren't exactly what you would call supportive.

It's one of those situations where someone is trying to publicly tear you down, but they say they're only joking when you ask them about it.

So, what was it that made him turn up out of the blue, slag me off on my Facebook comments section and message my friend telling her that I'd lost the plot and I had delusions of grandeur?

Who knows?

People have their own reasons for doing things; in the end I just deleted his ass off my Facebook!

If someone's either stabbing you in your back or constantly trying to belittle you then you need to get him or her out of your life!

It's not so easy with family members but at the very least, you'll need to limit the amount of time you're around that person.

This might sound a bit harsh to some people, but you need positive encouraging people around you if you want to achieve your goals and even more importantly if you want a healthy state of mind!

I love the film 'Limitless' because it explores the potential of the human mind and the possibilities for people if they open their mind, gain knowledge, and take action.

Bradley Cooper's character – 'Eddie Morra' is having a tremendous amount of success in a short space of time.

Ok, he's taken some sort of magic pill that opens up his mind so he can use his brain better than he's ever done before.

I can't promise that this book will be like the pill Bradley's character used in the film, but I can promise that if you have an open mind, this book can give you a push in the right direction to achieve some of your dreams and help you become the person you dream of being.

Because of Morra's success, he soon gets a meeting with Robert De Niro's character – 'Carl Van Loon,' who is a super wealthy investor. Van Loon asks Cooper, "What's your secret?"

Morra explains that his success was down to research, massive research and how mass psychology works.

Morra explains that he does have a formula for success and one of Van Loon's advisors cuts in and says that Morra has delusions of grandeur.

Morra says, "I don't have delusions of grandeur, I have an actual recipe for grandeur!"

This book will also provide a recipe for you getting what you want in life.

It's not the normal recipe book like Jamie Oliver produces and I probably won't say 'fuck' anywhere near as much as what Gordon Ramsay does.

Have I got all the answers?

No, but what I will give you in this book is some of the recipes I've used to become the person I once dreamed of becoming.

I once saw a clip on YouTube where Will Smith was talking passionately about 'not' being realistic.

He's right!

Everyone who has ever created or invented something awesome was a dreamer, had unrealistic expectations and was thought of by some, as having delusions of grandeur!

Now to contradict that slightly, I interviewed athletics world record holder Colin Jackson about achieving goals and his advice was to be realistic!

When I questioned him about this he said that when he started off in his athletics career, it wasn't realistic to assume he would break a world record in his early years.

So, who was right?

Was it Colin Jackson or was it Will Smith?

Well, they've both achieved international success at an extremely high level, and the fact is that both of them are right!

In other words, there is more than one way to achieve your goals; some people have different thought processes, some people have different techniques, but there are certain things that they all do that lead to success and I will explore some of these things in this book.

I'm not naturally brilliant at things and there are many things I can still learn and have much to improve on.

However, where I am now compared to where I was, is quite frankly...a fucking miracle!

CHAPTER 1

WHO GETS DELUSIONS OF GRANDEUR?

"I have a dream."
– Martin Luther King, Jr.

So, who gets 'delusions of grandeur?'

According to certain psychiatrists and psychologists it's people who are crazy.

Yes, there are people that are locked up in a mental facility who think they are a celebrity, a member of high society, the President, an army general or an important member of their community.

However, after many years of studying people who have achieved great things, I can confidently say almost all of the successful people I have interviewed or read about, all first thought they were more than their current circumstances showed.

They are:

- People, who were massively overweight but went on to build an awesome physique for themselves.

- People who had no money but went on to make big money.

- People who were useless academically in school but went on to build successful companies.

- People who didn't get any attention from the opposite or same sex early on in life but turned that around later in life.

- People who were overlooked by the teachers in school and later went on to teach others through public speaking and developed into great leaders.

- People who had little self-confidence but became super confident.

- People who were not gifted at athletics or sports but went on to achieve great things in those fields.

- People who thought they wouldn't be someone special, but they became the type of person that they once dreamed about becoming.

If you're anything like me and the people I've interviewed, you'll also have so called delusions of grandeur, crazy ideas, dreams and goals – but having these things are only half of what you need.

The next thing you will need to do to achieve your dreams is to take action!

Not random haphazard action, but precise, massive, kick-ass action!

You are already taking action by reading this book and even though you may feel good at the end of reading it, I sincerely hope that you take action towards your own dreams and goals.

Some people turn into professional students just by reading books or attending courses but sadly never take that next step to make their dreams come true.

Don't be one of those people!

CHAPTER 2

IS EVERYTHING POSSIBLE?

"To be or not to be, that is the question."
– William Shakespeare (from Hamlet)

Take a look back at your life and think about how things you once thought were impossible are now a reality!

Take a look at the technology that is around us today and take a look at the things you have achieved in your own life.

Many things that were impossible at first, are now not just possible but commonplace.

However, I'm not one of those people that think that if you believe you can achieve something, it will automatically become a reality, 100%, no questions asked.

The reason for this is because there are thousands, if not millions, of people who believed that 'one-day' their dream would come true, and for one reason or another it didn't.

We may not be able to make all our dreams come true, but what I do know is that if you believe something is possible, you've got a much better chance of making it a reality!

I'm also not an advocate of the phrase 'anything is possible,' somethings just aren't.

Example:

Swimming around in boiling water naked for a few hours and living to tell the tale.

Okay, somebody might develop a special swimming suit in years to come where you can swim around in boiling water, but I did say naked.

Maybe in a hundred or a thousand years from now someone will develop some sort of serum where your body becomes immune to the conditions around us, like some kind of Superman/Wolverine person.

As crazy as that may sound, there are already creatures on this planet that can live in extremely hot and very cold places.

One example of something that can withstand extreme temperatures is the Wood Frog.

Wood frogs are badass when it comes to surviving the cold for a long time. Scientists at the University of Alaska Fairbanks discovered that wood frogs use a substance called a cryoprotectant that is made up of antifreeze compounds and proteins which enable them to survive for over six months being chilled at an average temperature of -14.6°C (6°F) and could go as low as -18°C (0°F).

However, when it comes to the toughest, hardest, and most badass all round critters on the planet, the Water Bear (otherwise known as Tardigrade) is the King, the Daddy, the Don and Numero Uno of surviving so-called impossible elements!

This microscopic creature can survive temperatures as low as -273°C (459°F) and heat over 150°C (302°F) and you can currently find them on vacation in the depths of the ocean, Himalayan mountain tops, tropical rainforests, the Antarctic and mud volcanoes.

They can withstand pressures over 5 times more than the

pressure from the deepest ocean trenches.

They can survive radiation doses hundreds of times higher than the lethal dose for humans and can pop in and out of space for short breaks.

If they are in a place where there's no food or water – not a problem as they can survive for over 3 years without either.

Scientists from Oxford and Harvard universities looked at probabilities of Doomsday events such as a meteorite hitting the Earth, a supernova blast, and a gamma-ray burst.

They concluded that the Water Bear would probably survive such doomsday events.

At the time of writing, COVID–19 is sweeping through the planet and sadly taking many peoples' lives.

Spanish flu (also known as the 1918 flu pandemic) had an estimated death toll of up to 50 million people.

In-between 1347 to 1351, the most devastating plague in recorded history hit the world.

The Black Death, otherwise known as the 'Great Bubonic Plague' resulted in the deaths of an estimated 75 to 200 million people.

However, not even the Black Death could wipe out the Water Bear.

Astrophysicist Rafael Alves Batista told Casey Smith of National Geographic that the Water Bear species has existed for at least 520 million years and survived multiple mass extinctions!

Now that's one resilient little fucker, and I thought that grizzly bears were nails!

While all of this sounds very science fiction like, it's only a matter of time before scientists and inventors produce more and more things that were once thought of as impossible.

As we've gone from the horse and cart to the space rocket all within 150 years, it's getting harder and harder to say what is possible and what isn't.

Although it might sound a bit Jurassic Parky where they extract the DNA out of a preserved mosquito that's got a bit of dinosaur in it, and with a few scientists and a lab, they produce a dinosaur; who's to say that in a thousand or a million years from now (if the human race survives that long) this can't happen?

Maybe they'll be able to extract DNA from a water bear, cross it with a flea (that can jump 200 times their body length), cross it with a greater wax moth (who's hearing is 150 times better than ours and add a spider that can walk on walls.

For a bit of longevity throw in the atoms from the Methuselah (a pine tree said to be almost 5,000 years old) or perhaps even better, the Turritopsis dohrnii AKA the immortal jellyfish which transforms its cells into new types of cells and then goes back to an immature state!

In theory, growing old and young again; making the jellyfish biologically immortal.

Then you have what would be considered the ultimate thing to have...immortality.

Whether it's from the 1986 movie 'Highlander,' where immortals walk this earth looking to chop off each other's heads with swords that weigh about the same as a small buffalo. Or whether it's the 1989 Indiana Jones Last Crusade movie where Indie (played by Harrison Ford) is looking for The Holy Grail that you can drink from and gain immortality; immortality is right up there on many peoples Ultimate Wish List!

Just as the writers of Star Trek envisaged things before they became a reality, scientists, inventors, and other creative people are constantly making the impossible possible.

The question for us though, is what will become of our lives?

Will we achieve things that we can be proud of, or will we look back at our lives and be disappointed?

"To be or not to be," is something that we have more control over than what we may first think!

Everything that is man-made has come from someone's grand idea and the longer you live, the more you can appreciate what has changed and what advances the human race has made.

At the time of writing, I'm only 46 years old.

To children my son's age, I'm pretty old, but to some people, I'm just a young pup.

Either way, I've seen some amazing things happen over my lifetime.

The invention of the mobile phone, the MRI machine, the GPS, the laser beam, no not the one that kills people in James Bond movies, what use is that?! I'm talking about the laser beam that whitens teeth. What would our celebrities do without it?

In 1978, genetic engineering created the first synthetic 'human' insulin.

In 1998, we got the MP3 player and thank the heavens for the Zenith Radio Corporation and Eugene Polly who invented the TV remote control in the 1950's.

Even in my cars I've seen the changes over the years.

I got my first car when I was 18 because I'd had enough of driving from Wales to Scotland and half-freezing to death on my motorbike.

My first car was an old Ford Escort.

Yes it was a piece of shit that had wind up windows and a small basic engine, but I didn't care – it was something that I never had before so I enjoyed driving it towards Scotland until the police pulled me over and confiscated it.

Apparently you need a driving licence, insurance, M.O.T and car tax to drive up the motorway. Ahhhhh, the things you do when you're young!

As the years go by, you get these Gucci little things that we take for granted today like central locking, ABS brakes, electric windows, air-conditioning, and electric seats. In my latest car (a Jaguar XF), it doesn't even have a key (not too uncommon these days); you simply unlock the car with a key fob.

You get in and you push a start button that flashes like a snazzy red heartbeat. When you press that, the engine starts and a little round metal thingie (that's my technical name for it) for the gearbox pops up out of the centre console like something you'd see inside Dr Who's Tardis.

It also has flappy paddles on the steering wheel, so I can change gear if I want to drive it manually...amazing!

Think of your own first car, what was it like?

Even if you are only 17 years old today, you'll still be aware of some of the changes that have happened in the automotive industry over the years.

When I visited the car museum in Coventry it had a car there that you had to windup to start it, on the other end of the scale it also had jet-powered cars.

All of these things that seem quite insignificant now were once a really big deal.

When you have a big dream many people will be quick to think or say, "you have to be realistic," but if everyone thought like that we would still be living in caves and saying the words "ug ug" to each other.

Every material thing commonly available now was once thought of as impossible and unrealistic.

As I write this I'm looking around in my bedroom and looking at one of the simplest things in it. I'm going to say wallpaper is something that is fairly simple (at least compared to the TV, laptop, iPad and Samsung smart phone).

Today wallpaper is no big deal, but it wasn't around in the 13th century and was thought of as unrealistic and impossible to make back then.

To make the vinyl base for wallpaper you need stabilising powder, a lot of plastic pellets, solvent, the beaters, and you have to do many other things to make wallpaper.

Imagine you're standing in a cave or a forest and someone asks you to make a plastic pellet.

The chances are you have no idea how to make plastic, which is the same as me because I didn't have a fucking Scooby Doo how to make plastic before I looked at it on YouTube.

Apparently you'll need coal, natural gas, minerals, plants and crude oil to make it. Can you see my point?

Making something like plastic at one point was totally impossible and unrealistic but that's the way it is with any new thing.

Whether it's something material you want or something physical you want to achieve, there are people who will say that your goal is unrealistic.

They will think that you have delusions of grandeur.

However, if you have the right mindset, what may seem impossible for some people can become your reality!

CHAPTER 3

QUESTION EVERYTHING

"The important thing is not to stop questioning."
– Albert Einstein

If you believe that you're not destined for great things then you won't achieve great things but that's just because you told yourself you won't.

Don't get me wrong here, when I say achieve great things I don't mean you have to be the next Nelson Mandela or Mother Teresa!

I'm talking about what you think is great and what you would love to achieve personally.

If somebody else thinks what you're trying to achieve is no big deal then that's fine but it's also totally irrelevant!

If you want to achieve something then believe in yourself and go after it!

Just because you believe something, whether you've made up this belief or someone's told you what to believe, it doesn't mean that he or she or you are right!

It's the same, as just because you hear about something or read it; it doesn't mean it's true.

Here are some examples of what I mean:

Many people believe that bulls get mad when they see the colour red.

It's a common belief that bulls charge when they see red, but is this true or false?

To be honest, I don't really care, but apparently when bulls aren't being grabbed by the horns or fucking up China shops, they charge at anything that is red!

However, when Sky One's MythBusters programme did experiments with red objects, which included a life-size cut-out of a red man, they found that the colour red didn't make the bull angry.

What did piss the bull off was movement!

So, it's movement that makes a bull charge and not the colour red.

The expression, "As blind as a bat" has been with me for as long as I can remember.

So, is it true that bats are blind?

Not according to most online resources including National Geographic, who asked Rob Mies (Executive Director for the Organisation for Bat Conservation) if bats are blind?

Mies said this wasn't true and the larger bats can see three times better than humans!

If you ask most people in the UK (and many other countries around the world) where was Jesus born, they will probably tell you he was born in Bethlehem in a barn or in a stable.

However, when I went to Bethlehem, I was taken to the place where Jesus was supposedly born.

I was thinking to myself, how the fuck is that barn still standing after 2000 years!

They must have used some kick ass wood preserver made by God himself !

So, my girlfriend and me jumped on a bus and ended up in a tiny cave (that later had a church built around it) where Jesus was said to have been born.

To make matters more confusing, Christiananswers.net says that the Bible does not mention a barn, a stable or a cave. It only mentions a manger!

So, what is the truth?

To be honest I don't know – I wasn't there.

Will it make a difference to your life where Jesus was born? Probably not.

But it does give you food for thought and at the very least you can see that finding the truth isn't always as easy as you may first think.

So, what's the point of all this and how does it relate to you becoming more than you ever dreamed possible?

The point is, if you're anything like what I was, then you may not think that you're capable of becoming the person you want to be, and you may not think you will achieve the things you want to achieve.

Maybe someone tells you that you're having delusions of grandeur and you'll never achieve bigger things than you've already achieved.

Or maybe it's you that's always told yourself that you're not good enough?

Maybe once upon a time you were like me and you believed that bats are blind and bulls charge at red things, but all of a sudden you were presented with the hard facts and you changed your mind in an instant.

More importantly, you changed your belief in an instant and that is one of the goals in this book.

I know for a fact that you can become more than you have become, and there are still a lot of great things out there that you can achieve!

The placebo effect has been talked about and studied by many of the top medical professionals.

For those who don't know what a placebo is, it is usually a tablet or capsule, which contains no drug and is given to a patient to test whether the active drug works effectively.

According to www.nhs.uk, one well-known example of the placebo effect was done in 1996 where scientists got a group of people together and told them that they were going to take part in a new painkiller study.

The painkiller smelled like medicine, but it had no medicine in it, it was a fake!

Each student had the painkiller applied on one finger and the other finger had nothing applied to it.

Then each student had his or her finger squeezed in a vice.

The students said that they felt far less pain in the finger that had the so-called painkiller applied to it.

Their expectation and belief created real results even though the finger had no pain killing medicine on it!

The mind is an immensely powerful thing and your beliefs will create your reality!

The British National Health Service report went on to say: "placebos can get amazing results. The placebo is real and powerful!

The placebo effect points to the importance of perception and the brain's role in physical health."

The placebo is believed to reduce pain by changing people's perception and it releases the brains natural pain killer... endorphins.

Endorphins are released through exercise, laughing, sex and having quality relationships with friends and loved ones.

Having quality relationships with people comes down to how well you can get along with other people and getting on well with other people is something I plan to write about in a later book.

Endorphins have a similar chemical structure to Morphine – they lower stress levels, boost confidence, make you feel good and they give you a sense of peace and security.

When I was living with one of my ex girlfriends, I suggested that maybe she should try decaffeinated coffee rather than her normal caffeinated. She didn't seem too keen on the idea, but I convinced her just to try so she did.

I bought her the same coffee brand but just in its decaffeinated form.

After trying the decaf, she told me that she didn't feel as awake and that it didn't taste as good, so I put her back on the caffeinated coffee... or at least that's what she thought.

While she was out one day I bought her the caffeinated coffee but I did the ole switcheroo and tipped the caffeinated coffee into the decaf jar and I poured the decaf into the caffeinated jar.

Then one morning we were in the kitchen and I said to her, “I suppose you want your caffeinated coffee?”

While showing her the jar labelled as regular caffeinated coffee (that had the decaf in), she looked at me with a big smile, batted her cute little eyes at me and said, “yes please.”

She seemed happy that she was drinking her ‘so called’ caffeinated coffee again and a few days later I asked her, did it make a big difference being on caffeinated coffee. I also asked her if she felt more awake and happier in the mornings?

She looked at me with a big smile on her face and told me that being back on caffeinated definitely made a difference and she felt much better.

She had no idea she was drinking decaf, but because she believed she was back on caffeinated coffee, she felt better!

It's important that you question everything, especially your beliefs about yourself, if you are talking to yourself negatively and subsequently running yourself down.

The more negative things you say to yourself, the more negative things are going to happen in your life.

However, if you talk positively to yourself you can change your results, achieve far more in life, and live a much happier and fulfilled life!

When I was terrible at running I told myself that I was a good runner.

Of course, I didn't tell anybody else this because it just wasn't true, but after telling myself how good a runner I was over-and-over in my mind, I eventually became quite good at running.

So, before you write yourself off, give yourself a chance and tell yourself that you are brilliant at what it is you want to be brilliant at!

CHAPTER 4

YOUR DEFINITION OF SUCCESS

"Nothing can stop the man with the right mental attitude from achieving his goal; nothing on earth can help the man with the wrong mental attitude."

– Thomas Jefferson

This is without a doubt the shortest chapter in the book and I've made it that way for a specific reason.

It's short and sweet and I'm hoping it'll stick in your mind.

Ultimately, you have to know your own definition of success and everyone has their own definition of success.

Some people will define success in terms of money or fame.

Some people will define it as how many countries they've been to.

Some people define it as how much free time they have to do the things they love to do.

Some will define it as how fit or strong they are.

To some people, it's giving up alcohol or getting off drugs.

To some people it's being a great parent and for some people it's being given the 'all clear' when they've been battling a life threatening illness.

All of these things are success, but in broader terms, the best definition I've heard on success comes from Oscar winning actor Anthony Hopkins in a great interview with former ITN newsreader Martyn Lewis for Martyn's book, 'Reflections on Success.'

"Success in relationship to me, my own personality is about conquest, triumphing over, overcoming. Overcoming

adversities in oneself, limitations in oneself but also keeping a balance and I think a sense of humour about oneself, not making it the God but having a fair balance. That is it basically, in a few words...triumph, achievement, overcoming!"

Obviously, the words succeed, and success are closely related so let's take a look at the Cambridge dictionary to see how they define it:

'If you succeed, you achieve something you have been aiming for, and if a plan or a piece of work succeeds, it has the results that you wanted.'

In other words, know what you want out of life, follow your heart, and don't go chasing other people's definition of success!

CHAPTER 5

KNOW WHAT YOU WANT

"The only person you are destined to become is the person you decide to be."
– Ralph Waldo Emerson

When it comes to getting what you want out of life everyone has different ideas of what they want most.

The people who I admired the most were the ones that were super fit.

For me, the one thing that I wanted to be the most was super fit, which was, at that point in my life, not very realistic as my fitness was extremely poor when I was 16 years old.

Becoming an Army Commando was the first step on the fitness ladder for me and if you would have offered me a choice between becoming an Army Commando and a million pounds I can say, with my hand on my heart it was to become a Commando. That's how bad I wanted it!

Fuck big houses, fuck supercars, fuck travelling around the world on a yacht, I wanted to be an Army Commando and nothing, but nothing was going to stop me getting that Green Beret!

When you are that passionate about something, you put massive effort in and have an unbelievable determination... it's very difficult to stop you.

If you were in 29 Commando Regiment you were already very fit compared to most people but as high as the standards were in 29, there were two guys who (in my mind) stood out from the rest of us.

Their names were Ian Marsh AKA 'Marshy,' and Brian Davidson AKA 'Beastie.'

They were the kind of people that were legendary in 29, they could do things that not only normal people couldn't do, they could do things that most high achievers and elite military soldiers couldn't do.

I was in 7 Battery and was based in Arbroath, Scotland.

Marshy was in 79 Battery in Plymouth and then went into 148 Battery based in Poole. And Beastie was in 7 Battery and later moved to HQ Battery in 29 Commando's main base...The Royal Citadel in Plymouth.

Marshy later transferred to the Physical Training (PT) Corps and flew through the tests to get into the PT Corps.

The Chief Instructor on Marshy's PT course was Glyn Sheppard who by coincidence, lived in my hometown of Haverfordwest.

Glyn said that he remembered Marshy doing the test for dips.

I didn't ask Glyn what the pass rate was; I just assumed it be about 10 to 20 dips. Marshy did 130 dips and was still powering on when Glyn told him to get off the bar as he had to move onto the next test because of time restrictions!

Glyn said that Marshy went on to break most of the PT Corps physical test records.

Beastie's main claim to fame was winning the West Highland Way Race 3 times!

The West Highland Way Race is one of the world's longest established ultra marathons which first took place in 1985 on the long-distance trail between Milngavie (just north of Glasgow) and Fort William in the Scottish highlands.

The race is 95 miles which includes 14,760 feet of ascent.

All competitors must complete the race within 35 hours and there are many failures even amongst some very fit people.

Two days before writing these words I was talking to a guy who was in the UK Special Forces (SF) that attempted the West Highland Way race.

To get into UK SF, there are many tough endurance challenges which are responsible for the majority of failures.

It is said that on average 90% of people who attempt SAS selection fail the course.

Compare this to a tough challenge such as the Ironman where most people who enter it get through the course and an average of only 10% of the people that enter it fail to complete it.

The former SF soldier humbly admitted that he attempted the notorious West Highland Way run and never made it to the end (although he did manage a very respectable 70 miles).

I respected him for not only taking on the ultra run, but for also having the honesty to admit it was too much for him.

Of course, completing a tough endurance challenge is one thing, but being one of the best, if not 'The Best' is a whole different ball game!

Amazingly while running the course, Beastie's main fuel was Mars bars and when he finished the 95-mile race he would always hit the pub for a pint...fucking legend!

I remember watching Beastie and Marshy break the military marathon world record which is a 26.2-mile speed march carrying 40lbs.

When Marshy and Beastie did the military marathon world record they were part of a 29 Commando team and could only go as fast as the slowest team member because it was a team record.

I remember looking at them both when they finished the challenge, to my surprise they both looked as if they had just gone for a walk in the park.

I thought that was super cool and wanted to be just like them, but it didn't happen overnight, and it wasn't until I'd left the army that my fitness level went to a completely different level!

Knowing what you really want may sound like an obvious thing, and many people who leave school don't know what they want, I know this because I was one of those people.

I've also met people in their 20's that don't really know what they want to do with their lives.

Sure they'd like to be successful, but they have no idea what they'd like to be successful at.

This goes back to the classic analogy where a person without a goal is like a ship without a rudder where the ship randomly sails from one place to another hoping that it will be lucky and find paradise.

It is possible that you could bump into a paradise island on your random voyage, but it's very unlikely and nowhere as certain as if you were using a GPS or a map and a compass.

A friend phoned me up one day and said that the next step for me is to get onto the TV and have my own chat show, as I've interviewed many high achievers on my YouTube Channel and it's a natural next step!

However, the truth is I'm not that interested in being famous.

Of course there are millions of people out there who would love to be famous and there are those people out there that will do anything they can (morally or not) just to get into a national newspaper, the TV or the radio.

I would be a hypocrite if I said I'd never go into any of those platforms as I've already been in them.

It was only to serve a purpose of getting my message out there on a bigger scale rather than the whole, "hey look at me, I'm in the national papers etc..." There was a time when I did want to get into the national papers but when I achieved that in my 20's the novelty wore off really quickly.

I remember talking to one of my mates who was a bodyguard for some of the most famous people on the planet.

He told me a story about one of the top A-list celebrities he looked after and said that one day after work he went to a bar, came back to the celeb's house and the celeb asked him what it was like going to the bar?

My mate said he was slightly taken back with the question at first and initially thought it was a strange question to ask; he told him it was nice and thought nothing of going into a bar for a quiet drink.

Of course, the A-lister wouldn't be able to walk into a bar without people bombarding him for selfies and autographs.

So there are always good things and bad things about certain levels of achievement and you ultimately have to ask yourself the question, "what is it you really want?" because you have to take the good with the bad.

For me I have several things that matter more to me than the rest. Number 1 on my list is to be the most successful Daddy I can be to my son Léon.

To excel at being the best Dad mainly comes down to how much time I spend with him and how much quality time he gets from me.

With Léon mainly living with his Mum and Stepdad I don't get to see him everyday, but whenever I see him (usually every other weekend, every Tuesday after school and

Wednesday morning when I drop him off to school) he knows that he is loved. There are always lots of cuddles and lots of me saying things like, "Love you Léon," and questions like, "do you know who your Daddy loves more than anyone else in the world?"

To which he always says "Daddy," and I reply, "that's right; your Daddy loves you more than anyone else in the world."

I also make sure that Léon has good manners and is kind to people.

We can all influence other people; especially our children and they can often copy what we do.

The reason I am able to write a book on success is mainly due to my success in running but doing well in running is way down the list of importance for me compared to being an extremely successful Father.

You've always got to know what you want and if you're not getting closer to achieving your goal you may have to adjust, or you may have to keep going.

Not everything you put effort into works, but if you put effort into something you'll attract better results than you would without doing anything.

When there are roadblocks in life, it doesn't mean that you're not going to get to your main goals.

Just set goals and take action towards them, let go of the

outcome and put the work in.

Will the work always pay off ?

No, but at least you've tried, and you won't look back regretting that you never gave it a shot!

I was talking to a friend outside my house one day and he said that he couldn't run because he found it so boring, but at the same time he really wanted to lose weight.

I knew exactly how he felt as I remember going on the treadmill and doing a 10-minute run that I found very boring.

You may think that this was when I first started running, but it wasn't.

It was when I had already achieved many of my running goals and I had got out of the habit of doing consistent exercise.

The reason I found it so boring was because I had lost my 'why,' I had lost my purpose and I no longer had a strong enough reason to do it.

I had got comfortable and was no longer growing mentally.

My friend told me he was in a very dark place and he asked me if I could help him.

I explained to him I knew how he felt, and he said, "I'll give you a call sometime."

It is said that the road of 'sometime' leads to a destination called 'never.'

'Sometime' can lead to failure, but when you have a goal to do something in a certain time frame then you will be more focused, and you will get things done far faster!

When it came to write this book, I had no choice but to get on top of things. I had little time in the day to do things with everything else going on, but I had to make time.

The people that are the most productive and who achieve the most, often take on other projects and tasks even though they are already busy.

You can do far more than you think you can. It's like weight training.

Many times people hit a plateau with the weight they are lifting.

You think you can only lift a certain weight but when you try something heavier you often find that you can lift more than you thought you could.

It's the same with running.

Many people have a peak of 26.2 miles – a marathon. They think that a marathon is the ultimate they could do, when in reality, a marathon is just a distance set up by some other human.

It's very important to always visualise yourself as being successful!

The chances are you have already been successful at many things.

They don't need to be big things; a success is a success and you can build on that!

There are 'event' successes that don't happen very often such as a marathon or getting a diploma, which could take you years to achieve.

These long-term event successes are important.

However, an even more important success is the 'feeling' of being successful every day!

We need both in our lives, but we need that daily feeling of success and happiness the most because 'event' successes are here one moment and gone the next.

So when you want to feel successful and good about yourself, think back to some of the things that you've accomplished in your life.

Decide what you want to achieve and take action every day to achieve your goals!

CHAPTER 6

SEEING WHAT OTHERS CANNOT

"Every block of stone has a statue inside it, and it is the task of the sculptor to discover it."
– Michelangelo

A few years ago, I travelled to Rome with my then girlfriend to see the sights – the Colosseum, the Vatican City, the Sistine Chapel, and many other beautiful sights that Rome has to offer.

One of the things we saw was Michelangelo's Pietà and statue of David, which is the one that is stark bollock naked with a little winky and is perhaps Michelangelo's most famous sculpture.

However, out of all of Michelangelo's sculptures it was the Pietà that impressed me the most.

It was mind-blowing to me to see the incredible detail that Michelangelo had put into this sculpture of Mary holding the body of Jesus.

I was amazed how from a block of marble this masterpiece was created!

Michelangelo also said (referring to his statue of an angel), "I saw the angel in the marble and carved until I set him free."

It's the same thing with us, we need to discover who we really are and chip away at our rough edges to reveal the greatness that lies inside us.

We may be underperforming in life and we're not becoming the person we know we could be.

We think we're average and sure enough by thinking we're average we stay average, but inside us there is infinite power, we are more than we may be showing, and like the great Michelangelo we must have a vision; a vision not just of what we are trying to achieve, but also a vision of the person we dream of becoming.

To make our dreams a reality, it'll take time and we have to use the best information, systems, contacts and training that we can.

Sometimes you'll enjoy the process and sometimes you won't!

What is true of every great achievement you'll make in your life is that it'll take a lot of effort to achieve your goals and your vision!

But to achieve your goals you need to chip away bit-by-bit, day-by-day. This may be in the form of exercise, or a project you're working on.

With me, and this book, it's a case of doing things word-by-word, sentence-by-sentence, day-by-day and week-by-week.

If you're like me then you'll have days where you just can't be bothered to exercise, eat healthy, or do something that you know you should be doing.

Don't beat yourself up about it too much, all that matters is, "are you further ahead with your goals this year than you were last year?"

If you are, then good!

So, are you further ahead with your goals than you were last month? If you are, great!

Are you further ahead with your goals this week than you were last week?

If you are, brilliant!

Sometimes we need to take a break, but if we want to achieve more and we've taken a 2 or 3 year break; then maybe it's time to brush the cobwebs off our dreams and bring them back into our life.

Many people only believe what they see; if they cannot see something they cannot believe it.

Years ago, people believed things that weren't true.

For example, most people believed that the world was flat!

When we look at the world and the sky it seems that the earth is not moving but in reality our planet is spinning at roughly 1,000 miles an hour, so just because your eyes can’t see something it doesn’t mean that it’s not happening or it can’t happen.

In 1990, I left school and went out into the big wide world.

That very same year NASA launched the Space Shuttle Discovery, which carried the Hubble space telescope.

The Hubble was conceived in the 1940’s and built in the 1980’s.

What this tells us is that great dreams can take a while before they become a reality, so we have to look at the long term game plan!

We also have to be patient.

When you look at Hubble, it looks like a bunch of 6-year olds got together in a classroom with some cardboard from a toilet roll with tin foil and slapped the whole thing together, but no matter how it looks, the Hubble space telescope is a seriously awesome bit of kit!

The Hubble space telescope was built to see further than any other telescope so they launched it into space, which meant it couldn't be distorted with the effects of the Earth's atmosphere.

Much like the Earth's atmosphere that distorts telescopes from seeing what lies further; people also have distortions about how far they can really go.

In space, Hubble could see approximately 10-times further than telescopes on the ground.

When people look into space, all they can usually see is the blackness of space and stars but there is obviously far more out there than we can physically see.

Hubble can see everything from the formation of distant galaxies to the planets in the solar system.

The camera can see three different kinds of light such as near-ultraviolet, visible and near-infrared.

Just because, we can't see something, it doesn't mean it can't exist or it can't become a reality.

Many people won't be able to see your vision but if you have a dream you have to pursue it, because if you don't you'll end up being one of those people that has regrets and says things like, "if only I would have."

Have a vision of what you want, be willing to put the work in and go for it!

CHAPTER 7

THE EXPERTS CAN BE WRONG

"First they ignore you, then they laugh at you, then they fight you, then you win."
– Gandhi

In my book 'The Underdog,' one of the chapters is called 'Standing on The Shoulders of Giants' which talks about learning off experts and people that have gone before.

While this is generally good practice, there are situations when even the experts get it wrong.

So it's important to keep an open mind and think carefully about people saying what is possible and what is not possible and make your own mind up.

Many of the things we learn and many of the questions we have in life have already been discovered and answered by someone else.

This may seem like a bit of a contradiction, and yes a lot of the time the experts will be right, but there are times when you want to do something that is beyond the vision of certain experts.

But who are experts?

There are 2 main types of experts:

1. **Bluffers – those that think they're experts and we initially think are experts but aren't.**

2. **Those that are experts but can, on occasion be wrong.**

Let's have a look at an example of the different type of experts:

1. Bluffers

One day I went up to my local sports shop to get some new running shoes. As I was sitting down one of the salespeople came up to me.

He was dressed in sports kit and he asked me what I needed a new pair for.

I told him that I needed new sports shoes for running so without me saying any more on the subject he decided to give me his expert opinion.

He told me that the best thing that I could do was use a certain brand.

As soon as he said the brand I thought it was a bit suspect because it wasn't a well-known brand in the running world.

He took me over to the place where it said 'running shoes' and I noticed that the brand he promoted had more types of running shoe on the rack than any other make displayed there.

I could smell a rat!

There were hardly any of the usual players such as Reebok, Asics, New Balance, Adidas, or Nike on the rack.

I then asked him if the company that he was working for also owned this particular make of shoe.

He told me that they did. Bingo!

They were promoting their running shoe simply because they wanted not only to look better in the shop, but there would also be a considerable profit when they sold their running shoe.

In other words, the mark-up of the shoe from wholesale to retail was much greater, so it was all about profit rather than looking after the customer properly.

Nevertheless, the salesperson told me that these were still the best running shoes.

I don't go around telling everyone I bump into about my running experience because I don't want to sound like a twat and I simply don't feel the need to.

However, it had come to a head when I knew he didn't know what he was talking about and to be fair to him, he was probably told to tell customers that these are the best running shoes.

Trying not to sound like a dick, I told him about some of my running experience and then held the shoe he was promoting in my hand and told him why it wasn't a good running shoe.

It mainly boiled down to the shock absorption of this type of shoe.

I said to him, "No disrespect but can you get me the type of running shoe that I always use for running please?"

At this point he knew the game was up and he had to get me exactly what I wanted.

In other words, before you blindly listen to someone who labels himself or herself as 'an expert,' do some research first. We're lucky to live in a time where we can research topics and products on the Internet, so it's always good practice to research things before we believe what someone tells us.

2. Those that are experts but can, on occasion be wrong.

I first came across this when I was 17 years old and in the army. I was in Junior Leaders Regiment, Royal Artillery and my Sergeant Major asked me what regiment I would like to go into after I finish my training.

Even now I can clearly remember what happened. My reply to this question was, "29 Commando Sir." I'll never forget the look he gave me.

It was one of those looks as if to say, "There's no fucking chance you'll get into that regiment!"

Thank God he wasn't drinking anything when I told him; I think he would have spat it out.

In all fairness to him, he was a good guy and I think deep down he wished me all the best.

Right then and there I could have talked myself out of going for the Commando Course.

I could have said to myself, "Hey, this sergeant major is a great soldier with years of experience and if he doesn't think I'll pass this course, what's the point of even trying."

However, if we are to achieve our dreams, we must go after them, even if someone who we respect and who has a lot of credibility thinks we can't do it.

We may be wrong, but if we give it our best shot then we won't look back with regrets.

A great example of this is the Levi Roots story.

I had the pleasure of interviewing Levi after I saw him on the TV.

Levi had had a dream of selling his barbecue sauce on a national and international level.

He'd sold it for years locally and then decided to take a bold move and to go onto a BBC TV show called Dragons Den to see if he could get some millionaire investors to invest in his product to take his business further.

'Dragons Den' is a show in the UK and just like the TV show in the States called 'Shark Tank,' entrepreneurs pitch ideas to potential investors.

If the millionaire or millionaires like the entrepreneur's ideas they invest money and time in them.

When Levi walked into the room to pitch his product to the

wealthy entrepreneurs, he was playing a guitar.

Obviously, this is not a conventional way to do a proposal to investors, but it did make him stand out.

Unfortunately, as he told the potential investors about his plans he completely messed up the sales figures, so things weren't looking good.

Three of the millionaires that Levi pitched to didn't believe it was going to work.

The first possible investor, Duncan Bannatyne said, "Levi there's no business in this, I'm not going to invest."

The second possible investor Deborah Meaden said, "I think you've got a great business but it's for you and you will do well out of it, it's not going to be on a big enough scale for me so I'm out."

The third possible investor, Theo Paphitis said, "It's a hugely complex difficult business getting to major supermarkets. In fact I'd go as far as to say, you've got very little hope, so I'm afraid Levi, I'm out."

At this point Levi was probably thinking, "Fuck!"

The fourth possible investor, Richard Farleigh thought Levi's business skills would need some help, but he liked Levi's charisma.

And the fifth possible investor, Peter Jones said, "We know

how competitive this market is, it's almost impossible, I like impossible challenges."

When I interviewed Levi, we talked about his experience in the Dragons Den.

Levi went into the Dragons Den and asked for an investment of £50,000.

He eventually got the 50 grand off Peter and Richard for 40% of his company and they did make the so-called impossible possible.

Now 'Reggae Reggae Sauce' is in supermarkets all over the UK and Ireland. Sainsbury's were the first supermarket to take it on and expected the sauce to sell 50,000 bottles in its first year, but to their amazement it sold 40,000-50,000 bottles per week!

Levi also didn't do too bad and now has a net worth of tens of millions even though 3 experts said it would never happen!

Here are some other examples of experts not getting it right:

In 1878, a professor at Oxford University called Erasmus Wilson said, "When the Paris exhibition closes, the electric light will close with it and no more will be heard of it."

Professor Erasmus was a very clever man, but there are now billions of common light bulbs in use around the world.

In 1828, Dr Dionysius Larder, a science writer and academic

made the case that "Rail travel at high speed is not possible because passengers would be unable to breathe."

Today, the Shanghai Maglev Train reaches 268 mph during its daily service.

In 1876, senior executives at Western Union said, "This telephone has too many shortcomings to be seriously considered as a means of communication. It is inherently of no value."

According to staissta.com, in 2019 there were 931 million fixed telephone lines.

According to IHS Markit, in 2019 Apple shipped 193 million smartphones and Samsung shipped over 100 million more at 295 million!

And that's not to mention all of the other phone makes around the world.

Not including landlines, it is estimated that over 17 billion mobile phones have been sold since they were first introduced.

In 1895, Lord Kelvin, president of the Royal Society of Science, expertly argued that "Heavier-than-air flying machines are impossible."

But on 17 December 1903, the Wright brothers proved him wrong by inventing, building, and flying the world's first airplane.

In 1899, Charles H. Duell, Commissioner of the US Office of Patents said that "Everything that can be invented has been invented."

Since then more than, 7 million inventors have received patents from the US Patent office.

In 1903, Horace Rackham, the president of the Michigan Savings Bank advised Henry Ford's own lawyer not to invest in the Ford Motor Company.

He said, "The horse is here to stay, and the automobile is only a novelty."

According to worldometers.info, there are now over 1 billion cars worldwide!

In 1936, editors at the New York Times wrote, "A rocket will never leave Earth's atmosphere." Just 6 years later, the V2 missile, which was first launched by Germany, made it into space.

Less than 15 years after that, the Russians launched a rocket with the first satellite "Sputnik', into space.

In 1943, Thomas Watson, chairman of IBM said, "I think there is a world market for maybe five computers."

There are now over 2 billion computers connected to the Internet, which accounts for roughly 28% of the global population (at the time of writing).

In 1946, Darryl Zanuck, the founder of 20th Century Movie Studio and winner of 3 Academy Awards said, "Television won't last because people will soon get tired of staring at a plywood box every night."

Now, billions of hours of TV are watched each day from people all over the world.

In 1954, Dr. Wilhelm Hueper, Director of the National Cancer Institute, argued that, "If excessive smoking actually plays a role in the production of lung cancer, it seems to be a minor one."

According to tobaccoatlas.org, tobacco use has killed 100 million people in the 20th century, which is more than all of the deaths in World War 1 and World War 2 combined!

In 1959, IBM reported to the future founders of Xerox "The world potential market for copying machines is 5,000 at most."

While the photocopier is expected to become obsolete by many people, Xerox generated over $18.2 billion in copier sales, managing 60 billion printed pages.

In 1968, Time Magazine made the observation that, "Online shopping, while entirely feasible, will flop."

In 2013, worldwide online shopping reached nearly $1 trillion. At the time of writing, Goldman Sachs predicts year-over-year growth of almost 20% and life for me along with many of us wouldn't be the same without Amazon.

In 1969, Margaret Thatcher told an audience, "It will be years, not in my lifetime, before a woman becomes Prime Minister."

Ten years later she would prove her own prediction wrong by winning the 1979 UK general election.

In 1981, Bill Gates, founder of Microsoft prophesied the maximum speed of computers.

In his opinion he thought that 640K ought to be enough for anybody.

Today, the average personal computer is 300 million times faster than that.

In 1987, long-serving TV weather forecaster Michael Fish said that the BBC had received a phone call from a lady saying, "I hear there's a hurricane on the way."

Fish confidently told the British public, "Don't worry, there isn't." No prizes for guessing what happened next!

CHAPTER 8

MADE OF THE WRIGHT STUFF

"The moment you doubt whether you can fly,
you cease forever to be able to do it."
– J.M. Barry (Author of Peter Pan)

At the time of writing these words, I consider myself incredibly lucky to have travelled to 56 countries around the world.

For most of these journeys I flew by aeroplane, as millions of people have done. Today, we take the aeroplane for granted and even since the very day I was born the aeroplane was already in production, so to me it was just part of the society and part of the world I grew up in.

However, it wasn't always this way.

When people first had the idea of flying they come across huge criticism from others.

First of all, there was the subject of weight.

How could something that weighed a lot more than a feather possibly fly around in the sky?

Surely, this was impossible?

Today, the average aeroplane weighs several tonnes, but fly they do! Two brothers from Ohio had a dream of flying.

However, despite having good reputations for being kind and helpful people, when the public found out about their idea to build a machine that could fly, well let's just say many people thought the two brothers had lost the plot!

Neither of the brothers had finished high school but both brothers were skilled mechanics.

At this time people around the world were building gliders and were trying to fly.

The most famous person was the German Otto Lilienthal, who had experimented with over 2000 glider flights, but sadly one day in 1896 he crashed and died; his death made international headlines.

When the two brothers saw this they thought to themselves, well maybe we can create something that can fly?

The two brothers thought the best thing to do was to be able to control a glider.

Having already done a lot of work with bicycles they knew about controlling motion and their own research found that to fly aeroplane it would need to be controlled in three separate axes:

- Pitch (i.e. nose up or nose down)
- Yaw (i.e. left or right)
- Roll (i.e. rotates left or right)

Arguably, the most difficult to control of these three was the roll, so what the brothers did was study birds.

Birds are obviously the masters of flying, so it made sense to study how they moved.

This is no different when we want to achieve big things in our own lives.

We need to look at who has mastered what we want to do and emulate them!

The brothers noticed that birds change the angle of their wingtips to create a lateral motion, which is known as wing warping.

For the birds it obviously comes naturally, but the challenge was how would they put wing warping into one of their machines?

The eureka moment came to them one day when the brothers were working at their bicycle shop and a young boy came in and asked for an inner tube for his bike.

When one of the brothers pulled out the end of tube from the cardboard box that it came in, it gave him an idea of how the long flap-lidded box design could be used on a flying machine to deliver what they termed 'wing warping'.

They needed to build a glider with movable parts on the wings that could be altered to change its geometry, and thus, increase or decrease the lift that was needed.

For several years they experimented with small model gliders and then decided to build a glider that was big enough to carry a man.

By initially doing things on a small scale, this meant that the project costs were minimal, and when they had to adjust things and more importantly get airborne themselves, they would be less likely to get killed!

With our dreams and goals we often have to start off small.

If you started a fitness regime then you probably began by running only one or two miles rather than going out for a 10-miler at your first attempt.

It's a good thing to stretch ourselves but we also need to be careful that we don't risk too much, too soon and consequently crash and burn!

If you push your fitness too hard and too fast then there is a good chance you're going to come away with an injury and you're going to feel pretty negative about the whole experience.

It always makes sense to start small.

It's the same for when I started writing; I was over the moon if I could write 200 words in one day!

I could have never imagined that I would eventually get to a stage where I was consistently banging out over 3000 words-a-day, and sometimes up to 7000 words. So, set your goals small and then build on them!

In 1901, the brothers decided to test the glider and were willing to travel to wherever to pursue their joint dream as they needed a location that would provide strong and steady winds to increase the lift of the glider.

They came to the conclusion that Kitty Hawk in North Carolina was the very place they needed to be.

I have found that a willingness to go anywhere to further a project or yourself is something that is common with successful people.

They are not afraid to go to where they need to go to achieve the success they want to achieve.

You've got to be willing to get out there in the world, that way you'll come across many more opportunities than you would if you stayed in your local area!

Not only is travel important for success, I also believe that it's important to expand your mind and subsequently gain a worldly view.

You may not have to go up over 100 feet in the air to make your dreams come true, but the chances are you will need some bravery to a certain extent.

Anything that we believe in and want to pursue does require a certain amount of courage.

If you're a bit like me, you may not know exactly what you're doing when you start out on a new adventure, but sometimes it's just a case of experimenting and fumbling through until you get it right.

The good news here is the chances are if you make mistakes while pursuing your dream, you won't be killed like the brothers would have been.

Your ego maybe a little bit bruised but all you need to do is pick yourself back up and keep on moving forward!

When they experimented with their first glider, the brothers thought that would be the day they would solve the problem of wing warping and could fly like a bird, unfortunately, it didn't work out that way.

Another problem that they had was they couldn't create enough lift for the glider; and on top of that, one of the brothers was almost killed!

They almost quit the entire project but didn't!

When I started my quest to become an author, I can honestly say that there were times when I wanted to quit and never write another word!

However, with hindsight I can now look back at those early days and clearly see that I just wasn't committed, which is kind of like giving up without saying that you've actually quit.

If I wasn't putting words down towards a new book, or editing what I had already wrote then I wasn't getting any closer to producing a new book.

So if you're not taking action towards your dreams, nothing will change for you!

The brothers eventually fixed the wing warping challenge by replacing the rudder and then decided to build their own wind tunnel, which was a box about 6-foot long with a fan at one end that blew air into the box.

As I type these words, I'm thinking about how much the brothers got paid while doing their experiments.

The reality was, they had no big corporation giving them huge amounts of money, and they were just funding the project by the proceeds that they would make from their bicycle shop!

That's the same as many successful people.

They don't start off with a huge pot of cash and many people on their team helping them, they start off very small and build upon that.

Once you start producing results and people see that you're committed, then more people will support you and want to help you achieve your dreams.

Some people will need to be paid and some people will be inspired by what you do and just want to help out.

When I decided to commit fully to producing my first book 'The Underdog', I wasn't working as much as I could have worked, and the only work I did was to cover the bills.

Of course while I was writing I wasn't getting paid to write, but I didn't care because my dream was to become an author and that is what inspired me.

The brothers spent several months testing out different wing shapes to see which wing shape would be the best for lift.

After conducting lots of tests, they discovered that if they made the wing thicker at the front and thinner at the back it decreased pressure above the wing and increased the pressure below the wing, which would create lift.

In 1902, the brothers went back to Kitty Hawk to test the new prototype.

There were doubts but the glider worked brilliantly...it was a massive breakthrough!

One year later, they designed a glider with a petrol engine and they optimistically called the glider (with an engine) 'The flyer.'

The glider was made in their bike shop and they also designed the bespoke wooden propellers.

On 17th December 1903, a crowd of people watched in amazement as Orville Wright flew the first motorised plane!

The flight was only 12 seconds long, but those 12 seconds was so significant it changed the history of the world!

The brothers then flew an additional three flights with a combined time of roughly 60 seconds.

When the Wright Brothers built their first glider in 1900, the wingspan was 17ft 6in (5.33m). Its length was 11ft 9in (3.51m) and it weighed 52lbs (24kg).

I don't think even the Wright brothers would've believed that in 1988 an aircraft called Mriya and given the designation An-225 by Antonov (an Ukrainian aircraft manufacturer) would be built with the following specifications: wingspan 290ft (88.4m), length 275ft 7in (84m) and weight without fuel 628,317lbs (285,000kg or 314.158 tons).

It could also carry a payload of 545,000lbs (247,000 kg) in a commercial flight.

As you've probably already guessed the Mriya is the largest aeroplane in the world and also the heaviest aircraft ever that's ever flown.

I'm sure the brothers would also be interested to know that the official record for the fastest aeroplane in the world at the time of writing is still the Lockheed SR-71 Blackbird, which was recorded at 2,193 mph (3,530 kph) on the 28th July 1976.

Ever so slightly faster than the 19.1mph that Wilbur Wright recorded on the 14th December 1903 at Kitty Hawk.

According to the Daily Telegraph, in 2017 commercial aircraft carried nearly 4 billion passengers according to the International Air transport Association (That number represents individual journeys rather than unique passengers), which is nearly twice as many individual flights as there were 12-years ago!

Nobody has an exact figure for how many aeroplanes in the world there are today. Although, according to Ascend, who do aviation analysis, they estimate that there are roughly 23,600 aircraft currently in service with 2,500 in storage. The online publication Airliners.net estimates that there are even more. They estimate that there are around 39,000 planes in the world and throughout the history of the world there have been more than 150,000 planes!

The International Civil Aviation Organisation has said that the global air transport network doubles in size every 15 years.

At the time of editing this book, the COVID-19 virus is sweeping through the world and the airline industry has been severely affected.

However, it is widely believed that most of us will get through this and get back to normal life.

Whatever happens in the world from now on there is absolutely no doubt...Orville and Wilber Wright changed history when then invented the aeroplane.

So what were the lessons that we can learn from these incredible brothers?

- **Follow your dreams.**

- **Dream big.**

- **Don't listen to people who think you're crazy.**

- **If you didn't excel in school it doesn't matter. You can still achieve great things.**

- **Look at what someone else has done, learn from it and create something better.**

- **Shine in your chosen field by putting lots of time and effort into it.**

- **Look for opportunities in everyday life to achieve your goals.**

- **Start small and build on that.**

- **Be willing to travel to make your dreams come true.**

- **Take risks.**

- **Experiment with new ways.**

- **You will always make some mistakes.**

- **Things that you first thought would work may not work.**

- **If you fail, pick yourself up and keep going.**

- **Be committed.**

- **Don't quit, even when the going is tough.**

- **Take action.**

- **Use what resources you've got and make the most of what you have.**

- **If you persist you will eventually get a breakthrough.**

- **Doubts are natural sometimes – push through them.**

- **Be optimistic, believe in yourself and believe in your dreams!**

CHAPTER 9

TAKE ACTION

"Success seems to be connected with action. Successful people keep moving. They make mistakes, but they don't quit."

– Conrad Hilton (Founder of Hilton Hotels)

Action will always beat inaction!

Every time you don't take action towards something you want to achieve; you are slowly failing in life!

This can be all-sorts of things from asking a girl or guy out on a date, to getting sponsorship for an event you're planning, or writing your book.

Sometimes you may think that people who are happy and have a great life have nothing challenging happen in their lives.

It may look like it on the outside but all of us have challenges, and in many cases, people who live a successful happy life have more challenges than the average person when it comes to achieving goals.

They have often been criticised more, failed more, and put their neck on the line more than most people.

If you lose at something then try your best to take it on the chin, accept it with humility and don't beat yourself up about it all day long.

You are mainly in competition with yourself anyway and as I've said before, the greatest battles are our battles of the mind.

One person who always took massive action was Dame Barbara Cartland.

Her first book called Jigsaw was published in 1925 when she was only 24 years old.

Barbara Cartland had an incredible book producing system.

She first lay down on a sofa with her little dog and her secretary was placed to the right slightly behind her.

When she was ready Barbara would start talking. Her secretary would take shorthand notes of everything Barbara was saying, and the notes would later be written into a book.

There was also a tape recorder so not one word was missed. Barbara would start talking at 1:30pm every day just after lunch.

She was extremely punctual, and she believed that it was vital to start not at 1:35 PM or 1:40 PM but spot on 1:30 PM.

Along with her secretary, she was capable of producing 8000 words within the space of two hours.

While we are taking action and moving forward we always have a barrage of people giving us different types of advice.

Some advice is good, some advice not so good but ultimately when we push forward with things and see we've made a mistake, we can always adjust.

One of Barbara's policies was to have a happy ending in all of her books.

Her son said that she did produce one book that didn't have a happy ending and it was a complete disaster.

When the fans read the unhappy ending they sent Barbara letters from all over the world asking Barbara if 'Amy' – the main female character could marry the male hero at the end of the book instead of them being separated.

Barbara took her fans advice, changed the ending to a happy ending, which delighted her fans and they continued to buy her books in the millions.

The incredible thing about Barbara Cartland was even though she was so prolific with producing books; she was also a brilliant mother!

In other words, she always found time for her children.

In the morning she spent time with her children, in the afternoon she worked on her books and after she had finished working on her books she would spend teatime (around 5pm) with her children.

Barbara always used to say, "If you want to get something done then ask a busy person because they will get it done."

One of the things that I loved learning about Barbara Cartland was she was incredibly efficient with time.

After her secretary had written down Barbara's words, Barbara had 10 secretaries working with her reading, typing, and doing several other jobs.

She was interviewed on her 76th birthday and asked, "Why do you still produce books?"

There is no doubt that Barbara didn't need to do any more books, but she loved creating books and felt that what she was doing was worthwhile and other people enjoyed what she was producing.

Barbara's mother told her when she was younger, "When you grow up, you've got to do something in the world, you've got to give something, and you've got improve the world somehow."

Barbara said that when she produced lots of books she was criticised, and people would tell her that she did too many.

Some people said that they just don't want her books, which is fair enough, as different people want different things.

Nevertheless, she kept on taking action and produced 20 books in 1975, 21 books in 1976 and the year after it was 24 books.

According to her son, he doesn't think his father read any of his mother's books, which goes to show just because your partner isn't involved in your career; it doesn't mean they love you any less.

Barbara Cartland believed her vitamins contributed massively to her output and productivity.

She was also a fan of what was called back then, 'The health movement' and was a huge advocate of ginseng and vitamin B12.

Barbara Cartland was one of the most prolific and commercially successful authors in history!

She produced 723 novels, which were translated into 38 different languages.

In 1991, Queen Elizabeth II gave her the honour of becoming a Dame due to over 60 years of contributions towards society.

Many sources believe that she sold over 1 billion books!

The only authors to top this are William Shakespeare and Agatha Christie.

On 21 May 2000, at the age of 98 Barbara Cartland passed away at her residence in Hertfordshire, but she lived her dreams and died a happy, fulfilled woman.

She was a super-achiever, not only as an author, but, arguably even more importantly, as a parent, and that all boiled down to taking massive focused action!

More recently on 25 October 1984, a baby by the name of Catherine was born in Santa Barbara, California and was brought up by two loving parents who were Born-Again Christians.

From the age 3 to 11 years old, Catherine moved across the country as her parents set up churches where she also attended religious schools and camps.

She listened to gospel music and began to take singing lessons at the age of 9 where she started singing at a local church.

She also briefly studied Italian opera singing.

She loved music, started writing songs and started to play the guitar.

Catherine was taking massive action; she produced her first album, which sold 200 copies.

It wasn't going to set the world on fire, but she had achieved something she had never achieved before by producing the album.

Catherine was signed to two major record labels but was dropped by both.

Initially the record label didn't want her to come out with a song she loved. The reason for this was because they thought it was a bit risky and a bit too sexual.

As you can imagine her parents weren't fans of this either but in 2008 she released the song, which was called 'I kissed a girl' and it was a huge success!

She changed her name from Catherine Hudson because she didn't want to get confused with the actress Kate Hudson and became Katy Perry.

The rest as they say is history!

Catherine AKA Katy Perry became the first female artist to produce five number one Billboard hot 100 songs and she became Forbes top female earning artist for three years in a row.

How did she do it?

She took massive action!

She not only acted when things were going right for her, she also took action when things weren't going right for her.

So whatever is happening in your life, take action towards your goals!

Act when things are going well, take action when times are hard and even take action when all hell is breaking loose...just take action, action, and more action!

I was at the scooter park with my son Léon one day and another child said to his mum out loud in front of everyone, "you suck!"

His mum just stood there and took it on the chin.

I felt a little sorry for this mother but I didn't think she was handling the situation particularly well, so I said to her, "One of the best things I did in regards to bringing up my son was watching Super-nanny and Nanny 911. The people on these TV shows have had decades of experience in dealing with children with challenging behaviour. They had also achieved amazing results and have helped thousands of parents to get a loving more respectful household."

I told the mother of this rude child, If my son said that to me, I would give him a warning and say, "if you say that again to me you will be taken from the scooter park and lose the use of your scooter for at least 2 weeks!"

The mother said, "Yeah 'I SHOULD' watch that."

Watching or listening something is one thing and taking action on it is quite another, but of course you know when someone says, 'I SHOULD' you know that chances are they won't do it.

Maybe you've done this in your own life where you say, 'I SHOULD' because you think it will help change the quality of your life, but you don't follow through and take action.

Saying 'I should' is admitting there is a problem and you're not actively working on the problem.

What you say when you talk to yourself massively affects the actions you take!

When you catch yourself saying, 'I SHOULD,' turn it into 'I WILL' and then 'I DO' or 'I'M DOING!'

'SHOULD' is weak, 'SHOULD' is mediocre, 'SHOULD' or 'I NEED TO' is what holds you back and makes you lose out on your dreams in life!

That sort of thinking is only one level above 'I CAN'T!'

It's much easier to take action when you used the words 'I AM.'

For example:

I AM FIT

I AM A HEALTHY EATER I AM A GREAT PARENT

I AM BRILLIANT AT MY JOB

I AM VERY STRONG MENTALLY I AM A WINNER

Of course it's no good just saying these things and not backing these things up with the research and finding out how other people have been successful in their chosen field.

By learning the techniques used by successful people it will give you more confidence, and when you join the acquired knowledge with your new positive self talk you will take a lot more action and become much more successful!

Yes you have to override some of your old conditioning and let go of the past that you've been holding onto, but if you want to create new and exciting changes in your life, you have to think differently and do differently!

Most of us want a great quality of life.

If you want to create the life you want then you have to be

willing to put the effort in to get the great results.

If we see someone putting a lot of effort in, one of the expressions we use in the UK is... "He or she is a grafter!" meaning they are hardworking!

"If you want to create your dream life then you have to graft like fuck!"

One of the things that has been thrown around a lot in the last few years in the world of self-development is that successful people differ from the average person as they are willing to put in the amount of hours that is needed to become really good at something.

It has been said that to really excel in something you must put in over 10,000-hours into your chosen field.

I don't know how many hours I put in to running but what I do know is that I've put in more time and hours into running than most of the people I know.

For some people, running a marathon is a lifelong ambition, it's one of those things that many people do along with skydiving to tick off their bucket list.

Many people will read a magazine article that gives advice about running a half marathon or a marathon and take the advice from the person writing the article in that magazine.

A new marathon runner (or some that aren't so new) will train by taking the advice of running magazine articles but many writers give out a training program that makes the would be marathoner under-train and just get through the marathon rather than complete the marathon in a good personal time.

I guess a good time is all relative and just running a marathon is a great achievement for many people, but the reality is very often people can complete a marathon a lot faster and a lot more efficiently if they put more hours in.

If you're looking for a sub four-hour marathon then you could get away with a running 30 to 40 miles a week.

However, if you want to get a better time then you're generally going to have to put more hours in!

When you look at the elite marathon runners, they are averaging 100 – 120 miles a week.

Of course we're not all elite marathon runners, we don't all weigh nine-and-a-half stone (134lbs) like running legend Haile Gebrselassie and we haven't all got incredible genetics.

However, can most people run 100 – 120 miles a week? Absolutely!

Of course, no two people are the same and sometimes people get injured, or if they've just started running they won't be able to put in 100 – 120 miles a week.

That said; even if you put in 120 miles a week it doesn't mean you'll achieve a 2 hour 10 minute marathon like the elite runners, but what you will do is bring your time down quite considerably!

This is because your body is used to putting in the miles, but it's not only your body, your mind is far more used to it too!

On the flip side of that, when Ron Hill (who was the second man to break the time of 2 hours 10 minutes in a marathon) went over 120 miles a week in training, his marathon time was slower.

It has also been said that ultra-distance world record holder Yiannis Kouros trains no more that 80 miles a week.

So, where are the black and white statistics?

Surely, there should be a specific road map to the perfect training to get the best performance, right?

Well you would think so, but after much research on what makes the best the best, it seems that there is no one path to success!

Ultimately, you must listen to your body and if you constantly feel tired and drained then you'll need to take a rest, even if it's just for a day or two.

The same applies to work. If you feel mentally exhausted then you need to step back and go at a slower pace or take some time off work if that's possible.

So to summarise, 9 times out of 10 you will always get

better results if you put more time into something, but at the same time you have to experiment with this and listen to your own body and mind.

CHAPTER 10

FOCUS AND ADJUST

"Your life is controlled by what you focus on."
– Tony Robbins

In the year 2000, I decided to do a run in the United States taking in some great places and some iconic views.

The plan of action was to fly from the UK to Denver, Colorado and to start my run there.

When the plane landed, I got off, went through customs, walked outside the airport, made my way to a certain point in Denver and started running.

I hadn't slept much on the plane, but I wanted to start as soon as I could and didn't start running until late in the afternoon.

When I started running from Denver I had a goal to run 26 miles unsupported with a backpack weighing 45lbs.

I was carrying, spare clothes, my tent, a sleeping bag, wash kit, a gas cooker, dry food rations and lots of water.

I had carried this type of weight and heavier in my Army Commando days but there wasn't any consistent running so on the Commando Course it was at a much slower pace and usually a lot less miles were involved.

This challenge in the States involved much bigger distances and was tougher but I had matured, and my endurance was far stronger than when I did the Commando Course.

I didn't take into account that Denver 'the mile high city' had less oxygen than my home back in Cardiff, Wales.

I also thought that coming from Wales, I would be well

prepared for the hills in the Rocky Mountains, but the Rockies were on a different level and were tougher!

The combination of weight on my back, having less oxygen than normal and the hills took its toll on my body.

I was falling behind with my goal of running 26-miles a day and every day I fell further behind with my miles, which meant things were compounding over time.

Being behind just a few miles every day would eventually mean that by the end I would be hundreds of miles behind schedule and quite some distance off my original goal, which was 2,000 miles.

After only 3 days of running and carrying the 45 lbs I was having trouble with my ankles, they were hurting, and I was at risk of pulling out of my 60 day run after only 3 days!

Running 26 miles at my own pace was usually fairly easy and carrying a pack doing a speed march (a combination between jogging and walking fast) would have been ok, but the problem was the consistent pounding effect from running continuously up and down hills carrying the 45lbs.

On the 3rd day I had to make a decision on what to do, I knew if this carried on I would probably pick up an injury.

I had featured in the national newspapers, I had been sponsored with the flights to fly over to the States, I had planned, I had trained, I had prepared and the last thing I wanted was to get only three or four days into a 60 day challenge and have to fly home.

I wanted to keep my dried food I brought to the States, as I only had $150 to last me two months but the food and cooker added another 10lbs to my pack. I was down to the bare essentials, but I needed the rest of my kit and most importantly the water.

In the end the food and the cooker was the only thing I could get rid of, so I dumped them, if I didn't adjust and focus on how to get through the run I would have never made it.

I was stuck in another country for 60-days and I only had $150 in my pocket, which I knew wasn't going to get me very far. I blew through the $150 within the first week so I needed to adjust my strategy to get through the next seven weeks and focus on a solution to get food.

I was burning thousands of calories a day, so it was vital to get food inside me otherwise my energy levels would be depleted, and I would fail.

I ended up going into anywhere that sold food and asked to see the Manager, where I would produce an article of me doing this charity run in one of the national newspapers.

I'd say something like, "Hi I'm doing a sponsored run for charity across part of the United States, is there any chance you can sponsor me a Big Mac meal please?" Nine times out of ten I'd get food and that's how I got through the whole run.

Some people may have been mentally paralysed and wondering what the hell they were going to do with being stuck in a foreign country for nearly 2 months without any money or food.

This just goes to show that you must focus and adjust with whatever life throws at you.

It's no good sitting on your hands and bitching about what isn't going right in your life.

If there's a problem, there is almost always a solution, so it's vital to focus on your goal, adjust when circumstances change, and move forward!

In the end I got through the run, even after being bedded down for 3-days with a nasty case of the flu.

Because of the timeframe I had, I didn't do the 2,000 miles I'd hoped to do but I did cover 1,620 miles, which was far better than anything I had done previously.

My friend Dai Llewellin is a multiple British Rally Driving Champion and has beaten some of the top rally drivers in the world.

When he is racing around a course do you think he's focused on a wall, a tree, a hedge or is he focused on where he's going next?

The answer is obvious but how many of us focus on the negative things?

In other words, if your focus is on bad things then guess where you're heading next?

Yep, you guessed it, a little town in your mind called 'Shitsville!'

We all have challenges in life, and we all have things that go wrong but ultimately we need to get back on track by focusing on positive things and our destination!

Memories can be either unpleasant or nice to look back on.

For those people reading this that aren't on Facebook there is a feature on there called 'Facebook Memories' which lets you know what post you put up one year ago, two years ago, or however many years ago that you posted.

One day I saw a post I put that said:

"Wrote seven pages towards my new book last night, I think I can really get into this writing game. I'm also reading Phyllis Oostermeijer 'Choose Life' book!"

I was inspired by Phyllis, who is a local author and it made me think if a local living in my hometown can bring a book out, then so can I.

I'd thought about bringing a book out for years and had written some words many years before but I neither acted upon it nor pushed things forward!

So this was it, this was the start of me becoming a writing-machine and producing lots of books, right?

Wrong!

My first book 'The Underdog' was released in early 2017.

So why did it take over three and a half years for me to get my 1st book out?

One of the challenges was at the time it wasn't something that I really wanted to do. Of course it would be so cool to be an author and it would be even cooler to have a whole load of books out and supercool to be making a shit tonne of cash out of it!

I was struggling so much with writing that I needed to devise a new type of plan so I could get the words down and follow my dream of becoming a successful writer.

I needed to adjust and focus!

There are so many times during the day when other things would catch my attention and it would be easy to get distracted from writing.

Much of the time I'd rather be doing something else other than writing, as writing wasn't exactly my dream back then but having more of my books out was.

It was the same with my running, because I'm lucky enough to have two legs I do take it for granted and I have to say that while I am running I don't always enjoy it 100% of the time;

but I do enjoy the feeling I get when I've completed a run and I enjoy the results it gets me.

I've also noticed that even though I hated running to begin with, I do enjoy the process now and it became that way with writing.

One of the things that I decided to do was to put my dream in front to me.

Many authors write the book and get the front cover designed when the book is finished.

Personally, I find it much better when I can see the book cover in front of me, and then I have a goal to work towards.

I start looking around for things that could go on the front cover of the book and I start to use applications such as the poster maker app on Android to create a rough design myself.

After this, I give it to my designer Tom, who is a bit of a whizz-kid on the Mac and Tom tidies things up for me to make them look better.

After going through a few different colours and images I will decide on the final image and Tom will send me the finished design.

The reason I had these cover prints was that I could focus better and work towards completing these books.

The danger was if I didn't have the goal in front of me every day, then I could easily slip into putting it off, and it was for this very reason that my first book, 'The Underdog' took me over three years to complete.

I would routinely lose focus and many times, lose interest in writing the book.

I would drift off, do other things and by doing this I would go months and sometimes years without achieving goals!

The other thing I started to do recently is to have a certain photo of my son Léon in front of me.

The reason for this is because Léon is my biggest supporter and my greatest reason for writing.

More published books equals more inspiration for Léon and also more money, which helps us have a better quality of life.

He also asks me about my progress with my books and it was too disappointing telling him I hadn't done anything.

I knew I had to lead by example!

So whether I'm home, on a train travelling or if I'm in a hotel room, I've got his photo in front of me to remind me:

1. How lucky I am to have him.

2. That I need to focus and take action so I can create a better future for him.

Starting something off can be difficult at first but the more you do of something the easier it becomes.

I knew that because I produced one book I was capable of producing another, and if I was capable of producing two books then I was capable of producing three, and so on.

You've probably had something like this in your own life when you've achieved a goal and by achieving that goal you had more belief to achieve your next goal.

Of course when you achieve one goal you would be more likely to put the effort into achieving your next goal.

The phrase 'success breeds success' is true!

What I needed to remember was the reason why I was writing.

I needed to produce more books, to not only make my dreams and my son's dreams come true by making more money, but to help other people with their own specific path in life.

You need to write down your own dreams and goals and take massive action, because when you do this they are more likely to become a reality!

It's also a good idea to get people to help you with your goals.

When you've got a trainer or coach it can be of added benefit, because you're accountable to somebody, whereas if you just write your own goals down and don't tell other people and enlist help, you're only accountable to yourself!

Ultimately, everyone approaches things in their own unique way.

If something is not working for you, acknowledge what isn't working, focus on where you want to go, adjust what you are doing and take action!

CHAPTER 11

HABITS

"Successful people are simply those with successful habits."
– Brian Tracy

Most people don't realise how important habits are.

Everything you ever achieve will be based on your habits!

Habits can seem insignificant and you may think that they don't make much of a difference, but the habits you do every day will have a massive effect on how your life turns out!

Even if you have a lot of willpower, it alone is not enough to get you to reach your biggest goals in life.

Willpower is most important in the early stages of working towards your goal but when you combine willpower with habit, that's when your life can change!

In my first book 'The Underdog' I talk about the wires and the steel cables on a suspension bridge and related those linkages to your mental strength.

You can also relate the steel wires to habits.

The more you do those little daily habits the more they become like the little steel wires bonded together on a suspension bridge, which then turn into one large cable to create something magnificent.

Habits will lead you in a certain direction whether you are aware of your habits or not.

They can cause you to miss out on the good things in life, they can bring you misery and bad health problems, or they can lead to a better, happier, and more fulfilled life.

If you run most days you may not be lucky enough to break a world record, but I can guarantee that you'll be far fitter than if you did nothing!

So doing nothing and being lazy is also a habit.

If you smoke every day, you may not get lung cancer, but I can guarantee your health will be worse and your clothes and breath won't smell as nice.

If you lift weights every week, you may not become Mr. Universe, but you will be stronger and healthier than if you didn't lift.

If you eat lots of junk food and sweets every day, you may not die from a heart attack but it's far more likely you will put on weight and develop health issues.

Your daily habits create big results in your life and it's up to you to decide if those habits lead you to a positive or a negative result.

When I started interviewing successful people, that idea came from an initial step where I first asked someone for an interview, and then, I developed a habit of messaging someone new once a week.

Having messaged someone new twice a week, it then became once every two days, then I got to the stage where I thought I'd send out 2-messages per day and see what results I get back.

One day I sent over 30 tweets to high achievers.

I also got into the habit of looking for events that I could go to and find cool new people that I wanted to interview.

Did these habits bring results? You bet!

You only have to type my name into YouTube or go onto my Facebook 'Mark Llewhellin Tips On Success Coaching' page to see what results these habits brought in.

It's also worth mentioning that I've created another chapter in this book, which is called, 'If You Don't Ask' and specifically applies to how I ended up interviewing so many successful people.

There are many different factors when it comes down to being successful, but I can't promote enough that one of the very biggest keys to succeeding is down to your habits.

Training once or twice a week is usually harder for most people than training 4 – 6 days a week.

Why?

Because when you train at least 4 days a week it becomes a habit. It's just part of your daily routine.

It's who you are, it's what you do and it's part of your identity as a person.

You can often tell who's training and who isn't just by looking at them when they're wearing clothes that complement their body.

They put the effort in, they stand out, they look good and they feel better for it.

When it comes to daily tasks like walking up a set of stairs it's easier for them because they've done the cardio in the gym, in the hills or out on the road.

When they carry the shopping bags, it's easier for them because they've been lifting weights almost every day in the gym.

Of course you can get overweight people that train on a consistent basis too, but the main reason that they would be overweight is because of what they put in their mouth!

If you want to better control your eating habits then you've got to give yourself a good enough reason why you're not stuffing your face with food that will end up being detrimental to you.

For me, the biggest reason I eat reasonably healthy is because I want to be able to exercise with my son, and more importantly, I want to be as healthy for as long as I can be so I can spend as much time as I can with him.

Don't get me wrong, I'm still partial to a KitKat Chunky, a bag of crisps, a Chinese takeaway and a thousand other naughty but nice food types.

Let's also not forget to mention one of the greatest creations in the history of the Earth i.e. Ben & Jerry's Chocolate Fudge Brownie. It's yummy in my tummy!

All of this is fine, but fine in moderation. What is moderation you may ask?

There is an incredibly good chance that your body shape will tell you what the definition of moderation and excess is.

However, if you're like my mum and are the type of person that stays slim no matter what you eat; you also need to watch your cholesterol levels.

The late great motivational speaker Zig Ziglar said it best when he said:

"When you're tough on yourself, life is going to be infinitely easier on you."

One of the biggest things that I've learned in life is that the more time I put into something the better I get at it.

If we want to excel at something then we have got to be willing to put the time into it.

Sometimes we won't want to put the effort in, sometimes we just want to chill out and take time off.

There is nothing wrong with taking time off. In fact taking a break is a vital part of success.

The last thing you want to do is get to the stage where you are always tired because you work, work, and work!

But there is a fine line between taking time off so it can be productive for us and talking time off that it leads to never achieving our dreams.

We have to be careful not to let our focus slip, because if our focus on the goal slips we end up creating a new habit that can lead us away from our goals.

If I've done quite well in running, it's not because I was born a gifted runner, it's mainly because I focused on being a good runner, created a habit of running a lot, and put in more hours training than most people do.

So whatever goal you want to achieve then be willing to discipline yourself, be bold, take action and create a habit that will lead you to achieving your goals and your dreams!

So just to recap on the past few chapters:

- **Know what you want.**
- **Visualise what you want.**
- **Focus on what you want.**
- **Take action.**
- **Create a habit that will pull you towards your goal!**

CHAPTER 12

PRIORITIES

"Action expresses priorities."
– Gandhi

Life is a juggling act and you must juggle family, work, and social time altogether. This isn't always easy to do and sometimes you have to make decisions that you feel are the best for you.

The most important thing in my life is to make sure my son has the best life possible and for him to know that he is loved, no matter what he does or doesn't achieve in life.

Of course, I'm very proud of him when he does well at something, but the only thing he needs to do for me to love him is just be himself.

So for me, my time with my Léon is priceless!

Years ago, I was involved with a network marketing company and I listened to a guy by the name of Jerry Scriven, he talked about the importance of time and he said that some people will say one thing and do another.

He talked about an example of a guy drinking down the pub all the time.

The guy down the pub told everyone that his children are his priority.

Jerry pointed out that if he's in the pub all the time then the pub is his priority and not his children.

He then said a quote that has been credited to the philosopher and poet Ralph Waldo Emerson:

"What you do speaks so loudly I cannot hear what you're saying."

That's powerful stuff!

Many times people will say things and then do something completely different but will try to justify themselves and their actions to make themselves feel better.

Sometimes you must take a step back and take a good look at who you are and the actions you're taking.

Many people won't do that, they just drift through life kidding themselves and living a lie.

Many people feel helpless and doubt that they have the ability to change but the good news is that you can change, and you can become the person you dream of becoming!

Some people talk a good game, they 'talk the talk' but they don't 'walk the walk.'

They do little to make their life better and just complain about all the reasons why they haven't done anything significant with their lives.

I'm guessing that you're a little different because you've picked up this book.

You're probably the type of person that wants to make a difference in your life and you're the type of person that is more likely to walk your talk.

There's really no need to bullshit yourself or anyone else!

It only takes a little bit more dedication and work to live a happier more fulfilled life.

Is it worth it?

Well only you can decide that, but from my own experience with putting in the extra effort it has been totally worth it!

Juggling time with my son, writing this book, physical training, interviewing people (when I first started on this book), and putting on public speaking shows for my friend and business partner Mark Billy Billingham (from Channel 4's SAS: Who Dares Wins TV show) and everything else that goes on in my life hasn't always been easy.

Most of the time when it comes to being with my son Léon I've always put my work on the back burner, because for me spending time with him is more precious than any amount of recognition or money I will ever receive.

There is a point that you can get to in life when you realise the material things will never compare to having a connection to somebody very special, and wanting to spend as much time as you can with them.

Overall, Léon's mother has been brilliant. Sure we've had our little challenges but that's life and ultimately the best thing to do is to try and make things as good as possible for people.

Before the 2020 Coronavirus lockdown I saw Léon every other

weekend, every Tuesday after school and on Wednesday mornings I drop him off to school.

Sometimes we've had to juggle things around especially since 2015, when my life started to change more with interviewing successful people in London.

As I'm writing these words, I've got Léon on a Sunday night instead of having him on Tuesday night because I'm booked to go and interview a top adventurer by the name of Sean Conway, who was the first man to swim the length of Great Britain.

Sean is a hard man to pin down, but I had to take the opportunity to interview him whenever he was available.

There was a point where I almost cancelled it and just let things go on as normal just so Léon could keep to his routine but sometimes you must take these opportunities when they come up.

However, I'm always mindful and careful not to miss too much time with Léon, and if I miss one day with him I'll always ask his mum if I can have another day to make up for the lost day.

The trap many ambitious people fall into is when opportunities come up; they always take them and miss that precious time when their children are growing up.

It's not easy keeping a balance, but you have to decide what's most important to you, is it your career, your status, or your family?

Everyone has different views on this and I'm not saying what you should choose either way, but you have to think about how you'll feel in the future about some of the choices you make.

You don't want to look back on your life and think "If only I spent more time with my children or loved ones."

You also don't want to look back on your life and think, "I wish I would have taken that opportunity."

Keeping a balance is an incredibly challenging thing to do, but at the end of the day it's up to you to decide which way to go.

So why is there a chapter in a book about achieving big things talking about priorities with family?

The reason for this is that many books on succeeding focus mainly on money or becoming one of the best in your field – but if you only focus too much on money and status then your life will not have overall success and even more importantly...a healthy state of mind.

Most of us want a rounded success.

Pretty much all of us want happiness, health, successful relationships with loved ones, a certain degree of financial success and a good social standing; so we have to have prioritise what is most important to us, and make sure that

we are putting the right amount of time and effort into each individual priority.

That way we will live a happier and more fulfilled life!

CHAPTER 13

IF YOU DON'T ASK YOU DON'T GET

"Ask, and it shall be given you; seek, and ye shall find; knock, and it shall be opened unto you."
– Matthew 7:7

One person that is great example for asking for what you want and getting it is Richard Branson.

Branson has spent thousands of hours asking people for help.

Even though now he's in a position where he's the one that helps a lot of people, he still needs lots of help to keep his businesses running, and also, with setting up new projects and making more of his own dreams come true.

Even though some people think he had a lot handed to him on a plate, he has experienced a tremendous amount of rejection.

Rejection is just part of life no matter who you are, God only knows I've been rejected many times for lots of things, but you have to keep going and asking otherwise you lose out.

Although I'm confident that some opportunities will come around again, it's always better to ask.

Sometimes, you will get things without asking but most of the time if you don't ask, you don't get!

People that are high achievers will respect you for pursuing your dreams because they know the challenges you're going through.

They are also more likely to help you because they have been on a similar journey.

When I do something tough I never give much thought about

what people will think or say.

If it is something like an endurance challenge, then I am doing it because I want to see what I am capable of, and if I do it for charity it can raise cash for a worthy cause. That's good enough reason for me!

When you're on a path towards a goal and you want to attract things into your life the saying: "seek and ye shall find" is true.

Of course, you won't always find what you want, and you won't always get what you want, but by seeking and taking action you are far more likely to get the results that you want.

I decided to book a nice hotel on a weekend for a former girlfriend and myself and when we arrived and were impressed by the inside of the hotel.

It had undergone a huge refurbishment and the staff were kind and helpful.

The bedroom didn't disappoint either, my girlfriend was amazed by the girth and the length of the king size bed. So yes, size does matter.

We went for a meal and decided to pig out on a dessert, so we both went for the hot chocolate fondue with vanilla ice cream.

Most of the time when I'm at a fancy restaurant, I have to say that the dessert is usually a bit on the small side.

It's probably just as well, because more dessert equals more calories!

When the dessert came on this occasion, not only was it small, but the hot chocolate cake was only just above room temperature!

So, to my girlfriend’s amusement or horror (I'm not sure which), I sent it back and asked for it to be warmed.

I had already taken a bite out of it, so not wanting to be a diva and throwing my teddy in the corner, I ‘politely’ asked the waitress if she could slap it in the microwave for a few seconds and make it warm?

A few minutes later they came out with a new hot chocolate cake, “now that's more like it,” I thought.

I didn't care whether it was my old cake reheated or a new one!

All I wanted was the food described on the menu.

There are a lot of people who won't do what I did. In many cases, people will just make do and complain to their friends about the service or the product without giving the creator (in this case a chef) a chance to put things right.

You can’t please everyone all the time, but for me personally, I want to hear constructive feedback so I can make things better.

I like what Abraham Lincoln said;

"You can please some of the people some of the time, all of the people some of the time, some of the people all of the time, but you can never please all of the people all of the time."

If you want the good things in life you must ask, and when you ask, ask politely.

There are several little points to this story:

1. Ask for what you want.

2. If you don't get what you want, ask again politely.

3. Try to get things spot on the first time or you could waste your own time and get negative feedback from people.

One thing that came up was a Christmas charity dinner in Swansea with legendary rugby player Sir Gareth Edwards.

Swansea is only a short trip from where I used to live, so I thought this would be an ideal event to meet Sir Gareth and ask him if I could interview him.

I've found that people are much more likely to give you an interview if you meet them in person, and if you're already supporting an event they're a part of, even better!

I had also booked another interview later that same day in Cardiff with Nigel Walker the former Head of BBC Sport, who was also a former Welsh Rugby International and an ex-Team GB athlete, as well as being (at the time of writing) the Director of the English Institute of Sport (EIS) and thought I would have plenty of time to talk to both Sir Gareth and Nigel.

While I was at Sir Gareth's event I was sitting at my table thinking about leaving and meeting Nigel on time.

If I'm going to meet someone then that means they've scheduled me into their day when they could have been doing something else.

I always think about treating people how I'd like to be treated, so I'm generally very punctual.

As the Gareth Edwards evening went on, we all finished our meals and we were having coffee.

In my mind I was thinking, "Shall I go up to him while he's having his coffee, or shall I wait until he's finished his talk?"

I decided not to disturb him and wait until he finished his talk.

I thought his talk would go on for a short time, but I was wrong!

As brilliant as the talk was I remember sitting at my table thinking "I've got to go and meet Nigel now" and I knew I was pushing the time by waiting as long as I could.

In the end, I had to leave the room while Gareth was still on stage talking.

I got to Nigel's house just in time and the interview with him was brilliant, but I kicked myself for not seizing the opportunity with Gareth when I should have!

I was even more frustrated after because I had met the event organiser Mandy at the very start and complimented her in putting such a great event together.

Mandy was sitting right next to Gareth and all I would have needed to do was to go up to Mandy while they were having coffee with a smile on my face say, "Mandy this event is awesome (Bearing in mind Gareth was sitting right next to her and would have heard me say that!),

I would love to stay but I've got to go and interview Nigel Walker (Gareth would know straight away who I was talking about)."

A bit of name-dropping goes a long way because:

1. They know or are familiar with the person.

2. It gives you more credibility.

3. Many people think, hey, if you're interviewing this person on their tips for success, I've achieved a lot; I'll give you my tips!

I guess you could call that a kind of an ego thing, but the

truth is almost everyone (including myself) likes people that acknowledge them for who they are and what they've achieved. I was listening to a guy, who claimed that he has no ego at all.

He was basically saying that he was so spiritually advanced that he's dropped his ego altogether.

That was something that made me smile, because the fact that he said those words showed that he still had an ego.

Not to mention he was on a popular TV show, he has sold millions of books and he goes on speaking tours all over the world.

The point is, everyone, yes even highly advanced people like Jesus, Buddha and Gandhi would like people to listen to them, follow them and take what they have to say seriously.

Another point to the story was, seize the moment!

Sometimes you may not think the timing is right, and you may be fearful that you'll look a fool.

However, if that is the only chance you'll get, just go for it and ask.

What's the worst that could happen?

It's just like asking a girl or a guy out.

If you don't succeed with that person you can simply move

on to someone else...NEXT!

The story doesn't end there.

I kept pursuing my goal of wanting to interview Sir Gareth and eventually (through my friend Darryl Jones) it happened.

We even became quite friendly; having tea at his house several times and Sir Gareth came to one of the talks, which I produced and hosted for Billy.

So, sometimes opportunities can come up again.

There's a fine line between acting too soon by seizing the moment and being patient and waiting for the right time for something to happen.

Ultimately, what is meant to be is meant to be, and all you can do is your absolute best!

Just keep on asking for what you want, be persistent and I can promise you that most of your dreams will come true and you will create an incredible life for yourself, and the people close to you!

CHAPTER 14

KEEP GOING

"Success is stumbling from failure to failure with no loss of enthusiasm."
– Winston Churchill

There will be many things in your way when you're trying to achieve something and sometimes it's just a case of persisting and never giving up that will get you to reach your goal.

One day I was invited to meet the Jordanian Ambassador by Sailing Champion Tracy Edwards.

I didn't have a shirt to wear for the event, so my mate lent me a nice pink one.

It fitted me ok, but the only challenge was it needed ironing.

No big deal I thought, so I got the iron out of the hotel cupboard, turned it on and waited for it to heat up.

Unfortunately, it was broke!

I phoned the reception for another one, but I was extremely pushed for time at this point.

I had no idea how long the hotel would take to deliver the iron so rather than wait for the hotel to bring one up I decided there was a quicker way to get an iron.

I began knocking on doors in the hotel so I could ask someone to lend me the iron in their room.

With the first door there was no answer, with the second door the occupant was in the bath, so that was a no too! I tried the third, fourth, fifth, sixth, seventh, eighth and ninth but there was no reply!

I kept going and was starting to run out of rooms to ask on my floor when I saw someone going into his room, so I said, "Hiya mate, sorry to bother you but my iron is bust and I'm in a rush to get somewhere.

Any chance I could quickly borrow yours please?"

He kindly gave me his iron; I quickly ironed my shirt and made it to the event on time.

Of course this is just a little example of taking action, asking, and never giving in but whether it's a small goal or a big goal, persistence makes the difference!

How many people would have asked someone to borrow an iron?

Not many!

Most people would have waited around for the hotel to bring up the iron, even if that meant them being late.

Maybe that's just my punctual military training kicking in (always be 5 minutes early for an appointment and all that stuff!), or maybe it's that I think it's polite to be on time when someone has invited you to something?

The point of the story is asking, and persistence works!

I'm yet to come across someone who has succeeded in something big by not being persistent.

Yes, there are people who have been lucky with certain things and have been handed things on a plate, but the high achievers of this world are persistent and keep going until they get the result they want.

Some people are amazed how many incredible people I've interviewed, and I'm often asked how I got these people to agree to do an interview.

The truthful answer is...I asked, and I kept asking.

I know many people think that it can't be that easy, but it simply is.

When I started interviewing people years ago, the world record holder for the high hurdles was Colin Jackson and I really wanted to interview him.

So, the way I went about it was to tweet him using Twitter.

No reply!

About a month or so later I sent another tweet, and again still no reply.

Several months later, I was asked to go to a charity dinner and was subsequently put in the VIP section, and guess who was there?

Yep...Colin Jackson!

Earlier on in the year I had attended a running event that

Colin had organised. In the event they handed out T-shirts that said the name of Colin's charity, 'Go Dad Run.' Now what T-shirt do you think I wore to the charity dinner?

Yep, you guessed it! It was the 'Go Dad Run' T-shirt and when Colin saw this he was delighted.

I was introduced to Colin by my friend Cheryl Hicks and asked if he would be up for an interview sometime, to which he said yes. Bingo!

It took months after that to make the interview happen, as Colin's schedule was so busy.

However, eventually we set up a day for the interview and agreed to meet in a coffee shop near the motorway.

I knew a busy coffee shop wouldn't be the best place in the world to interview people because of the noise, and I wasn't sure if they would let me interview him there.

So, before the time of the interview I decided to arrive early and do a little recce of the area.

The only place I could find that would let me do the interview was a gym that was being built.

It was a bit of a mess and it was a little bit like a building site inside, but it was the only option I had where it would be quiet.

I also coincidently met a guy in the coffee shop, who I had

recently met at another charity dinner. He said that if the gym didn't come off then I should give him a call and we could use his building for the interview.

An hour or so later Colin arrives, we have a coffee and then I tell him I've got a location to do the interview.

We walked over to the gym and to my horror I found that they had locked it up!

The owners had decided to leave the building, which left me in the lurch, and I was now standing outside with Colin and my cameraman (Kristian Kane), looking at me.

I put on my bravest face, smiled, and said no worries; "I'll get another place now."

In the meantime, Colin was left standing outside with Kristian which was not good!

I thought to myself, no problem, I can phone this guy who offered me the building and Plan 'B' will come into effect.

So, I'm now standing outside ringing this guy in front of Colin and Kristian and guess what, he doesn't answer the phone; Plan 'B' has gone... what we call in the UK, "tits up!"

Now I'm going to have to make up a Plan 'C' on the spot!

I went to one building and asked them if I could use their building to interview Colin, but they told me that they couldn't give that decision without the Manager being there and he wasn't on site.

Time for Plan 'D'...the next few buildings I went to were unoccupied and locked!

Plan 'F' was a wine shop.

I told the guy in charge about the situation and said, "I have Colin Jackson waiting outside and I really need a place to do the interview please?"

I asked him if I could use the Manager's office and he said that it wasn't possible because it was a bit messy in there but he did tell me there was one place they could let me use.

Brilliant I thought!

I got Colin and Kristian and made our way into the wine shop; because of the way things were going I decided to offer Colin a bottle of wine.

This wasn't a great situation either because I knew I hardly had any money in my bank account at the time; which meant if he picked a very expensive bottle of wine it would've been very embarrassing for me when the cashier tells me my card has been declined.

Colin didn't go overboard, and he picked a £12 bottle of wine, so I was grateful that he didn't go for any Dom Pérignon or Cristal, because if he did, I would've been completely fucked!

I ended up interviewing Colin in the wine shop's store

cupboard.

It was a far cry from the BBC studios and the prestigious studios around the world that Colin is used to, but it was better than nothing.

To his credit, he never moaned or complained about a thing and did a brilliant interview.

In the end I made the best out of an awkward situation, so the moral of the story is;

Never give up and if you don't ask you don't get!

CHAPTER 15

LUCK

"My success was due to good luck, hard work, and support and advice from friends and mentors. But most importantly, it was dependent on me to keep trying after I have failed."

– Mark Warner

Luck is a subject that is talked about a lot in the world of personal development and many people who have achieved things on a high level will say the old cliché, "the harder I work the luckier I get" and will want to take all the credit for succeeding! While there is a lot of truth in that, the full truth is that there is more to succeeding than just putting in hard work.

If you were born in an extremely poor country, with a brutally controlling government and you had severe mental or physical disabilities, I think you'd agree that it's harder to succeed?

The most honest high achievers will tell you that they did put a lot of effort into making their dreams come true, but they will also tell you that there is an element of luck to their success.

Just before I wrote these words, I was watching David Letterman interviewing George Clooney and they both acknowledged that there is a lot of luck involved with their success!

I can't say that I'm a natural writer but becoming an author was a dream come true for me.

When I was 16 such a thought was simply impossible to comprehend! I mean come on, a kid that didn't do well at English in school becoming an author, what are the odds on that?

However, what I will say is that becoming an author was

mainly down to putting the hard work in with a combination of luck!

The luck part was now mainly because I could now self-publish my books via platforms like Amazon, Apple, Kobo, and many others.

I once heard a quote from a guy by the name of Dexter Yeager, who was a car salesman and later became a huge success in the Amway network marketing business.

Dexter said, "If the dream is big enough, the facts don't matter!"

It's a good quote but there are certain circumstances where no matter how big you dream; your goal will not come true.

For example, you may play the lottery and have a big dream that one day you'll win the biggest ever jackpot.

However, something like that is mainly down to luck.

There may be someone who dreams about winning Wimbledon, but if she or he is a double arm amputee, it's not going to happen!

You may have someone who has a big dream that one day they'll break the 100m sprint world record, but they don't have the fast twitch fibres in their genetics, so it's not going to happen!

However, in a broader sense of the quote, Dexter is still right to an extent.

If the effort you put in matches the dream that you have, then there is a much better chance that you'll make that dream come true!

Even if you never become the best in your chosen field, you'll still be a lot further ahead in life and closer to your dream by putting in lots of effort than you would be if you didn't give it a shot!

Although I wasn't a natural runner and went on to do well with running, there was a lot of luck involved in that too!

Yes, I put in far more hours on the road than most people would, so I'll take the credit for that!

What I can't take the credit for is that I was very lucky not to have serious injuries, which could have stopped my running.

Sure, I've had loads of injuries that have taken time to get over.

Foot injuries, ankle injuries, calf injuries, knee injuries, shin injuries, hamstring injuries, hip injuries, you name it, I've had most of the injuries you can get with running, but they've all healed.

Some people I know are disabled or have injuries so bad that they can never run again, so you bet I've been lucky!

What have you achieved in your own life by putting in hard

work?

At the same time you may also know that you had a bit of luck with achieving that goal.

Myself, and my son Léon used to play WWE wrestling on the iPad, it's a game he loves and to be honest at the time I got a little bit addicted to it as well.

We also started to watch some of the wrestling competitions on YouTube and one night I was watching a young WWE fan by the name of Connor 'The Crusher' Michalek, a 7-year old who had cancer; his hero was the WWE wrestler Daniel Bryan, so of course his dream was to meet Daniel.

Thanks to some amazing people Connor was invited to WrestleMania and his dream became a reality.

When Daniel met Connor he said, "Connor was special for one million reasons, his smile, he was so quick witted and nice to everybody.

You couldn't help talk to him and instantly fall in love with him."

Daniel Bryan went on to win WrestleMania and guess who he went to see first when he got out of the ring – little Connor.

Daniel leaned over to Connor and hugged him and said to him, "Connor you mean a lot to me, you give me a lot of strength; you've helped me earn this and please keep on fighting."

Connor's dad said Connor was elated!

One day Connor's Dad Steve got the most devastating news any parent could get, there wasn't much time left for his little angel and Connor sadly died in 2014.

There are many things that increase your chances of getting cancer, which include smoking and drinking alcohol.

Of course Connor was too young to do any of these, so he couldn't be blamed for getting cancer.

The truth is any child, or anyone for that matter could get it!

What is the point of this story you may ask?

The point is;

If you made it to adulthood you are already incredibly lucky and always be grateful for what you have got!

CHAPTER 16

JET POWERED DELUSIONS

"Great spirits have always encountered violent opposition from mediocre minds."
– Albert Einstein

While visiting my (then) girlfriend in Warwickshire one day, I decided that I would look around for things to do in Warwickshire while she was at work.

This is when I came across the jet powered 'Thrust SSC –the fastest car in the world,' which was on display at Coventry Museum of Transport.

Many years before I had sent an email to the man that made this possible – 'Richard Noble, I told Richard about my dreams and goals and he was very encouraging and supportive.

As I've mentioned before, big thinkers are far more likely to encourage you because they are the type of people who know they have made their own dreams come true.

I knew that Coventry had a massive part to play in the field of transport many years ago. What I didn't know was that the man that invented the jet engine was born in Coventry.

It seemed a fitting place for Thrust SSC to rest, as not only was Coventry the hub of the car industry but the jet engines mounted on each side of the car were invented by somebody who also came from the city.

During the time of World War 1 a young boy was at home obsessing about machines and especially the newly invented aeroplane.

This young boy had seen the aeroplanes being built and saw one crashland near his house!

Despite that, his dream of becoming a pilot was moulded at a very young age and he passionately wanted to join what would become the Royal Air Force (like my good friend Paul Hughes, who is one of the main editors of this book).

It was reported that the young man physically wasn't up to much, as he was a very short person and initially the Royal Air Force didn't want him.

However, the young man persisted, and he eventually achieved his dream of entering service with the Royal Air Force.

He quickly became an incredibly talented pilot and as a natural risktaker would always push the boundaries of what the aeroplanes he was flying could do!

As much as he loved flying, he believed that planes could be made much better.

He believed that they could be faster and travel further, but he needed to come up with an idea that would revolutionise aviation.

Of course, when some people found out about this, they thought that he had delusions of grandeur.

The young man's name was Frank Whittle!

Whittle knew that the lower the altitude that the aeroplane was flying at, the denser the air, which subsequently increased the drag factor.

So, he wanted to come up with a way of making aeroplanes not only fly faster and further, but also higher.

Quite simply, if aeroplanes flew higher it would be far more fuel efficient due to the notably lower drag.

One of the challenges with flying higher was that the higher the aeroplane would go, the less oxygen there would be to run the engine efficiently.

Not only that, propellers needed more air to 'bite into' to move the aeroplane forward. While other inventors were thinking about how they could make propellers better, possibly with different materials, bigger or smaller blades and the shape of the propellers, Whittle believed that the plane needed something completely new.

After working on his new propulsion system Whittle got a breakthrough and was invited to meet one of the top aeronautical scientists of the day, A.A Griffith.

For Whittle's dream to become a reality, he needed the support of Griffith and the British Government.

Whittle showed them a design, which showed an engine with a fan at the front that sucked in air and compressed it in a combustion chamber.

Then fuel was sprayed into the chamber and ignited.

Whittle believed that the burning gases would propel the plane up to speeds up to 596mph.

Unfortunately for Whittle, Griffith told him that it would never work and refused to help fund the project.

This was a major blow for Whittle, as he looked up to Griffith and believed that his design would work.

Griffith was dismissive of Whittle's idea and there is no doubt in my mind that Whittle would've been devastated by such a rejection.

Griffith said that there was no metal in the world that was strong enough that could stand up to the intense heat in the combustion chambers and the engine would melt!

At that point, many people would've turned around and called it a day, but Whittle believed in his invention, he believed in himself and if anything, it made him more determined to produce the engine that he wanted.

Whittle didn't have the backing of the British Government, but he was resourceful and despite that door being shut to him, he made moves to open up other doors and get private funding.

He then spent the next eight years working on his invention.

It took a lot of time, a lot of patience, a lot of determination and a lot of persistence!

In 1937, Whittle was ready for his prototype engine test.

It was a huge day for him but unfortunately it ended up not

going to plan and the test failed.

Whittle wanted to be the first person that invented the jet engine but there was competition from other nations, especially Germany.

At the time Adolf Hitler made the jet engine a priority.

The Germans also had a prototype and they installed it into a German fighter plane. On 27 August 1939, the aeroplane took off and was a success, but only to a degree. The flight lasted only six minutes because the metal couldn't withstand the heat of a jet engine.

Only a month later Hitler invaded other countries and triggered World War 2.

Initially, the British Government didn't consider the jet engine enough of a priority, however, now that Hitler had invaded Europe, they knew they needed the best technology available.

Although the British Government wouldn't support Whittle at first, they changed their mind.

Whittle was given the necessary public funds by the Exchequer and was put in charge of a team of the best available engineers.

The next plan of action would be to get metal manufacturers to come up with a metal that would withstand the extreme temperatures of the jet engine.

Although there was no one metal that was strong enough the

manufacturers finally developed a mixture of chrome, nickel, steel, and molybdenum.

Many times in life, you either have to join certain components together or join forces with other people to produce the best results.

Not wanting to shy away from testing prototypes, Whittle climbed into a Gloster Pioneer plane on the 11th April 1941 to conduct some ground tests.

A day later the decision was made to put another pilot in the plane to test the jet engine off the tarmac.

The aeroplane flew for 17 minutes before it landed safely back on the ground; this was a massive success, not only for Great Britain but also for every other country in the world!

While I was doing research on who invented the jet engine, there were several people in the comment section saying that Romanian Inventor Henri Coanda invented the jet engine (like they were there when it happened).

Although, yes, I'm British and it would be quite biased of me and quite normal to say it was a fellow countryman that invented the jet engine, I really don't care. I wasn't there, so I don't know 100%.

Who invented what, and when, isn't that important, and it certainly won't change yours, or my life.

However, Sir Frank Whittle's design was and still is the

blueprint for the jet engines today!

The lessons we can take away from this great man are:

- **Have big dreams.**
- **Persist.**
- **Take risks.**
- **Push your limits.**
- **Think of new ways of doing something.**
- **Even when someone you respect rejects your idea; it doesn't mean that you are wrong.**
- **If you are rejected, still push forward if you believe in your dream.**
- **Be resourceful.**
- **When one door closes, another one opens.**
- **Be willing to invest a lot of time into your dream.**
- **You will always have competition.**
- **People that once wouldn't support you could support you at a later date.**
- **Join forces with others.**

EPILOGUE

With finishing off this book, I'd just like to say a few last words to you.

I've spent a good portion of my life striving for dreams that I wanted to make a reality.

Sometimes I've succeeded and sometimes I failed. But for the most part, I have achieved far beyond my wildest dreams.

They may not be wild dreams or big achievements compared to what other people have achieved.

However, when I think back to when I was that 16-year-old boy with little confidence and didn't believe in myself, I know I've come a long way.

The point of saying this is that I know if I can go from where I was to where I am today then I know you can achieve great things in your life!

Many people first thought I was totally off my rocker and they believed

I had no chance of achieving what I have now achieved.

When you want to achieve something greater than you've ever achieved or you want to become more than you currently are, you're going to attract critics.

My recommendation to you would be to keep your dream in your mind, get good people to support you, write down your goals, focus on where you want to go, read or listen to positive books or music, put the work in, take the setbacks on the chin, keep moving forward and eventually you'll get there!

"Here's to the crazy ones. The misfits. The rebels. The troublemakers. The round pegs in the square holes. The ones who see things differently. They're not fond of rules. And they have no respect for the status quo. You can quote them, disagree with them, glorify, or vilify them. About the only thing you can't do is ignore them. Because they change things. They push the human race forward. And while some may see them as the crazy ones, we see genius. Because the people who are crazy enough to think they can change the world, are the ones who do."

– Rob Siltanen.

HAPPY

Finding Happiness In A Crazy Ass World

MARK LLEWHELLIN

INTRODUCTION

"When I was five years old, my mother always told me that happiness was the key to life. When I went to school, they asked me what I wanted to be when I grew up. I wrote down happy. They told me I didn't understand the assignment, and I told them they didn't understand life."

– John Lennon

With this book I decided to home in on a subject that is one of the most important to most human beings; the subject of happiness.

I think you'll agree, there's nothing in this world that is more important to your life and the lives of the people you love than happiness.

Happiness is right up there with health in terms of what is most important in our lives!

So, if happiness is one of the most important things to master during our lifetime, then why isn't it on the national curriculum?

I doubt very much if you've ever been taught anything on the subject?

Throughout your whole time in school you probably didn't even do one lesson on it!

Zero, nothing, nada, zip, zilch, not one jot, diddlysquat, jack shit… sweet FA!

One of the things that most people want in life is happiness, but very few people learn about happiness and how to be happier.

Why?

It's like society has a belief that you are either happy or you're not and that's the end of the story.

However, I believe that if you want to excel at something then you're going to have to learn about that very subject.

From my own perspective, if you have a natural talent for a particular thing you can always improve by learning more about it.

Sometimes you'll see people who always seem to be happy both publicly and behind closed doors.

They walk down the street with a smile on their face and look as if they don't have a care in the world!

Happier people have more doors open for them, they're luckier people, they walk around with a spring in their step and a glint in their eyes.

Other happy people walk around with a quiet, calm confidence and when the shit hits the fan in life, many of those people have the ability to handle it better mentally!

Happier people also don't get ill as much and when they do get ill they usually recover quicker and have more energy and vitality in life!

So here's a question, are you happy at least 95 – 99% of the time?

If you are, that's fantastic!

If you're not, then you're selling yourself short.

You're not only selling yourself short on a daily, weekly, or monthly basis, you are also selling yourself short with your entire life!

I'm a happy person most of the time, so I decided to do a self-analysis and delve into why I'm happy most of the time, and then write it down and help others, so this is how the book you're now reading came to be.

Throughout this self-analysis, I kept asking myself the question, "Could I be even happier and if so, how?"

Of course there are obviously times in life when I'm not happy.

I'm still a human being and I still have emotions like most other people, so I can still be emotionally hurt and experience sad and unhappy times.

When I've lost family that are very close to me, it wasn't as if I was in the hospital next to the deathbed opening a bottle of bubbly and celebrating.

Although, I might have been if I was left with a very large inheritance… I'm joking!

If you have people that you love dearly and have lost, you know exactly what I'm talking about.

For over 25 years I have done research on psychology, philosophy, and personal development so I could become happier and more successful in different areas of my life, and

I'm still learning new things.

Doing this has made a massive positive difference in my life and I've achieved some pretty cool things, but even more importantly than any of my achievements, I've been lucky enough to be happy most of the time too!

Can you train your mind so that you can be happy 100% of the time?

From what I've learned about people, it's possible to be happy most of the time, but to be happy 100% of the time is highly unlikely, and if there is an individual on this planet that has been happy 100% of the time, I have never come across them.

In order to be happy 100% of the time you would have to:

1. Never have been hurt mentally.

2. Never have experienced any physical pain.

Without wanting to sound pessimistic or negative, the chances of anyone not experiencing these two things as they go through life is zero!

That's just reality, and it's part of the deal we're all given while we're here on Earth.

Let's face it, there'll be some challenges that you'll go through in life that will be as welcome as a turd in a swimming pool!

There will be times when you'll get totally blindsided by life!

One minute, your life is going great, and the next minute, everything turns into one epic shit show!

This can be anything from losing the job that you thought was secure, losing a relationship that you thought was going well, or it could be the loss of a loved one just to name a few things.

Whatever you go through in life, the most important thing is to get back on track and find happiness in your life!

Like you, I certainly prefer to be happy more often than not.

Also, I realise we all have different lives, and I am only one person, so I have limited experiences and there is still much that I have to learn in life.

To that end, I not only use my own life experiences in this book, but I also draw off the experiences of other people and have done extensive research on the subject of happiness to provide you with the best information that I can.

In this book, my goal is to help you get out of your negative mindset when you feel down, and to help you shift over to a more positive mindset that will lead to a happier and healthier life.

We're all unique so there's not one set of rules for all, just like there's not one set of rules for every person losing weight.

Running and eating heathy is one of the best ways to lose weight.

However, if you have arthritis in your knees, or if you have no legs, you'll have to find a different form of exercise (although eating healthy will always work), you'll have to find what works for you and it's the same with happiness.

In other words, simply take out of this book what works for you.

There is no one definitive guide to happiness; there is only a guide because we are all different!

Not only that, the world is constantly changing, and as we move forward we will all have unique experiences in life.

Also, just because this is a book on happiness with the lovely smiling emoji on the front cover, it doesn't mean that we're not going to get down into the nitty-gritty of things that need to be addressed.

It's not as if nothing bad will ever happen in your life.

We all know that's not the reality.

In other words, your life has either:

"Just come out of a shit storm, you're currently in a shit storm, or you're heading into a shit storm!"

It wouldn't be right if I simply fluffed over the challenges that we'll all face with happy, happy, happy words in this book, without addressing the realities of life.

There is only so much I can put in this book about finding more happiness; however, you'll find more information on the subject of happiness throughout certain chapters of almost all of my personal development books because of the importance it has in our lives.

My goal with this book is to make a positive difference to your life.

I'm hoping that you'll discover a few things in this book that will add to the overall quality of your life and make you a happier person; I feel that if you take one positive thing from this book and it makes you happier, then this book has served its purpose and writing it will have been worthwhile.

"The most important thing is to enjoy your life, to be happy."
– Audrey Hepburn

CHAPTER 1

HAPPY GENES

"Make the best use of what is in your power and take the rest as it happens."

– Epictetus

Ok so let's start at the beginning of what can affect happiness.

One thing that we have to factor into our happiness is: how much of our happiness is to do with our genetics?

Is it God given or luck?

And if genes do play a role in our happiness, how much so?

The website PositivePsychology.com reported that a meta-analysis study conducted at Stanford University showed the role that genetics play in depression.

It concluded that an absence of depression is not an indicator of the presence of happiness.

They also studied the 5-HTTLPR gene which showed that the more people that have this certain type of gene (which is a serotonin transporter gene), the higher the levels of satisfaction and happiness they have.

Another study from the Minnesota Twin Registry reported that 50% of life satisfaction boils down to genetics.

Many other studies report that 40 to 50% of our lives and subsequent happiness stems from our genetics.

I did consider writing a longer chapter on genetics, however there was simply no point because at the end of the day, what we've been given, is what we've been given, and we have to make the very best of it!

Moreover, many people will try to use this as a crutch.

In other words, if genetics are responsible for 40 – 50% of our happiness, many people may feel as if their happiness is out of their control. This could push their unhappiness up to levels of 95% or even 100% because they will use it as an excuse.

And if you're like me or 99.9% of the population, the chances are you've never even been tested for this gene, so you won't even know.

So to what amount do the things that happen to us in life contribute towards our happiness?

This is ultimately down to the individual as we're all different, and different situations affect us all in their own unique ways.

The exciting thing is that you can grow stronger mentally through learning and understanding how your thoughts work.

If I can become excessively strong mentally and happy (most of the time), then so can you!

However, if you want to succeed at most things in life, you'll have to put the time and effort in. I have spent over 25 years putting time and effort into learning about psychology, happiness, and personal development!

I humbled myself by learning from the people that have gone

before me and it's changed my life in the most amazing ways!

When you feed your mind with this type of information, you're not going to turn into some terminator type machine, or any other kind of robot, in which you have no emotions.

There will be times when you will still get really hurt and are unhappy.

However, with time and patience, you can learn to become a phenomenally strong person mentally and get back to happiness quicker than ever before!

For most of us, our starting point as a baby was shortly after we were born.

What is one of the first things that babies do when they are born?

There aren't many babies that are born with a big smile on their face and full of the joys of the world!

Nope, most of us are bawling our eyes out and are extremely upset!

So, if we're not crying in distress like we were on the day we were born, then there is only one way to go… And that way is up!

CHAPTER 2

THE "I'LL BE HAPPY WHEN" STORY

"Plenty of people miss their share of happiness, not because they never found it, but because they didn't stop to enjoy it."
– William Feather

You may have fallen into the trap that millions of people, if not billions of people throughout history have fallen into.

They have fallen into a trap of believing that they'll be happy when they reach a certain goal.

However, the reality to this way of thinking can unfortunately lead to a lot of misery along the journey because you're more focused on the current situation you're in and not where you want to be!

Have you ever told yourself, "I'll be happy when... (fill in the blank)"

I know I have.

The ironic thing about that type of thinking is, when you reach your goal, it's usually satisfying for a brief moment, and then you decide to set your next goal, and think to yourself, I'll be happy when I achieve this next goal!

Before you know it, you're like a little puppy dog chasing its tail, trying to catch something that you'll seldom catch.

Even if you do catch it, and experience that brief moment of happiness, many people let go of that happiness because they're after their next goal and won't be happy until they reach that goal.

Does this sound familiar?

The 'I'll be happy when' story we make up in our own minds

is a classic bullshit story that we often tell ourselves, which by its very existence cuts out 99% of the happiness throughout our entire lives.

Crazy isn't it?

Sadly, many of these people aren't even aware what they're doing, which shouldn't be the case for us after we've read and digested these words.

I have a coffee mug that says:

"Happiness is not a destination, it's a way of life."

When the COVID-19 pandemic hit in 2020, many countries around the world got shut down to one extent or another and many people had to stop going to work.

Some people loved it, and some people hated it.

For some of the ones that still had accommodation and could still afford to eat, many of them decided to embrace the change and the slow pace of life if they were furloughed and therefore off work.

Many of these people decided to enjoy not having to get up in the morning and be at work at a certain time.

They decided to enjoy their families more, they decided to enjoy their free time more, and they decided to enjoy nature and life a lot more too!

It was as if they had suddenly come out of the rat race and didn't give a shit about who had what! They simply enjoyed what they had in life.

In other words:

"If you're too busy to stop and appreciate everything that you have and everything that you've achieved, you will never be happy, and you will have failed in one of the most important areas in life!"

I've written a book called 'Grab Life By The Balls' (which hasn't been released at the time of this book getting published) which talks about living life to the full; it also incorporates surveys about what people want most in life and their regrets.

I won't go into the specific details in this book as I've covered it in 'Grab Life By The Balls' but this point is still worth mentioning:

One of the top regrets people had when coming to the end of their lives was that they felt they had worked too much!

This next quote sums it up nicely:

"When all is said and done, success without happiness is the worst kind of failure." – Louis Binstock

Just before I started writing this part about enjoying the journey and being happy in the present I was playing on my son's wrestling game.

I know… here I am, an ex Army Commando and bodyguard and I'm playing on games that were mainly designed for children to play.

I even remember listening to some of my friends talking about playing these types of games and thought, "you're in your 20's, 30's and 40's, I can't believe you're playing these games at your age," funny how things turn around sometimes.

At one time, I did get a little bit hooked on playing a superhero game called 'Injustice' on my iPad.

Sometimes we get hooked on these things, and we do certain activities as a way of avoiding something that we should be doing to move us forward in the game of life. This was something I ended up doing and this is something we need to be aware of.

I was telling myself that playing this game was vital because I could win Léon some more characters for his games, which was really a load of crap!

I did feel a sense of escapism in which I got the feeling of going back to being more like a child, not having to be concerned about the stresses of adult life, where you're in a world governed and judged to a large extent by status, money, achievement, taxes, and control.

However, there also comes a point where we have to deal with these things, take our head out of the sand and face life's challenges head on.

As I've said just before writing this piece, I noticed that I was playing on Léon's wrestling game just for the sake of building credits and getting a new character for him (or so I told myself!).

I actually got to the point of not enjoying what I was doing; I was more focused on getting the prize than enjoying the game and this is what we often do in life.

We are so obsessed with the end result that we stop living in the present and enjoying the now.

We all dream about possibilities for the future whether it's that new car, the new house, the dream holiday, or the latest gadget that we want, but it's important to enjoy the journey because that's what life is made of!

On the subject of Léon and his games, he was playing a game called 'Subway Surfer' and after every game he said to me, "have we got enough coins to buy someone new Daddy?"

Like many other games you win coins by doing well in the games.

At first I didn't mind him saying this, we all want to make progress of some sort in our lives, but this got to the stage where he was asking if we had enough coins after every single game.

After the fourth or fifth game I had had enough of this question because he was focusing too much on the next new thing and not enjoying the character he was playing with.

I asked him not to keep asking me this question (as he was about 100 games off winning a new character) and to simply enjoy playing the game.

Yes it's good to get the reward at the end of the game, but he needed to enjoy the journey as well.

So it wasn't just an adult challenge, it's also something children go through too.

If you've got to a stage of focusing on the next thing all the time and no longer enjoying the moment, then stop and think about how much time you're wasting.

You're literally wishing your whole life away!

So remember, it's great to have something to look forward to, but enjoy the moment as well.

Also, if you take the right steps and enjoy the moment, while you're putting the effort into achieving your next goal, the chances are you will have achieved that next goal before you know it, as time will have flown by!

One of the things I love about running or cycling, when you're not in a race, is that the journey can be a lot more important than the destination.

The destination can be great, and you can be happy that you've got to your destination, but most of the time you'll be working towards your next goal, so it would make sense to find things to be happy about right now, rather than just being happy at one point in time when you've achieved that goal.

In summary:

Don't become a bore and take life too seriously, stop to enjoy the little things!

"Learn to enjoy every minute of your life. Be happy now. Don't wait for something outside yourself to make you happy in the future. Think how really precious the time is you have to spend, whether it's at work or with your family. Every minute should be enjoyed and savoured."
– Earl Nightingale

CHAPTER 3

THINK POSITIVE THOUGHTS BEFORE YOU GO TO SLEEP

"Very little is needed to make a happy life, it is all within yourself, in your way of thinking."
– Marcus Aurelius

The scientific study of dreams is called oneirology. Dreams mainly occur during the 'rapid eye movement' (REM) stage of sleep, when our brain activity is high, which resembles the state of being awake. Just in case you were wondering, yes, the band, R.E.M. was named after this dream state condition.

According to research, we have between 3 to 7 dreams a night.

Even though we have many dreams while we're asleep, it's the dreams that happen just before we wake up that are the dreams that we remember.

Have you ever had a dream, and you woke up straight after that dream and was able to remember that dream?

One morning, I had just woken up after a dream.

Unfortunately, this dream was far from pleasant; it was more of a nightmare than a nice pleasant dream.

In this dream, for some reason the police were after me because of something to do with computer hacking a big business.

All I remember was that I was being treated like this major computer hacker who had done something, and they were waiting for their opportunity to arrest me.

I remember thinking in the dream, do I go on the run and try to avoid them, or do I just hand myself in?

The dream led to a scenario in which I was on my way to an appointment, which I knew they would've known about.

I also knew this was the best opportunity they had to arrest me.

It wasn't long after that I woke up.

As I woke up, I could remember feeling upset, disappointed, and as though I had failed in life.

The interesting thing about this was it felt real, I mean really real!

Of course in my real world none of this was true (especially the part about being clever enough to be a high-level computer hacker), but regardless of it not being true, I truly believed it was until I woke up and came back to reality!

How many times do we think about something, or worry about something that isn't even real?

I know I've done it many times in the past, and when you think about it, it's a little bit crazy because that situation isn't happening, but you think that it might, and you start to feel bad about it or upset about it.

You're visualising something going wrong, and of course that never makes you feel good, which in turn makes you feel unhappy.

A lot of this has to do with an inbuilt system that we have, which is passed down from our early ancestors and is just trying to protect us.

So, trying to override that basic human system isn't the easiest of things to do, but we can do it if we focus and concentrate enough on positive thoughts.

When a negative thought comes into your mind, it is important that you immediately replace it with a positive one.

This takes self-awareness and a conscious effort to put this into practice.

All too often we go into autopilot, which makes us feel bad, and if we stay on autopilot and don't consciously take charge of the controls of our mind, we'll keep feeling bad on a regular basis, which can ruin our lives!

For me, to wake up feeling unhappy and scared about a situation was extremely rare, and it made me think why this had happened.

Why did I wake up frightened I thought to myself?

I traced it back to the evening before where I had been watching the TV and had come across several negative stories, which were very tragic.

Because those stories were one of the last things on my mind that evening, I went to bed with negative thoughts.

However, those negative thoughts didn't end as soon as I

went to sleep, there was a very good chance that I dreamt about them more than once in the night, and of course, when I woke up in the morning, I was still stuck in a negative mindset.

One of the stories was about the spread of the COVID-19 virus.

It talked about how many people it had killed and the mess that the economy was in as a direct result of the pandemic.

Another story was about American basketball superstar Kobe Bryant and his daughter getting killed in a helicopter crash.

Before I woke up from the dream about the police being after me and realising that I was looking at a long prison sentence, I also remember having a dream about the helicopter crash.

It wasn't a clear dream, but I can remember the dream feeling very real, and it was as if I was in the helicopter looking on as a spectator.

So, what's the moral of the story?

Focus on positive thoughts before you sleep.

When you wake up in the morning, you are likely to wake up with the thoughts you had just before you went to sleep.

For example, three positive thoughts I often have before I go to sleep (at the time of writing) are.

1. How grateful I am to have such an amazing son.

2. I am so grateful to live the lucky life I live.

3. I also tell myself that I'm a successful and highly prolific author, because it is one of my main goals at the time of writing these words.

Let's look at some negative things I've thought about in the past.

Maybe you've thought similar things:

1. I can't believe that person did that to me!

2. What a mess my life is in!

3. What if I lose (fill in the blank)!

It doesn't take a brain surgeon to work out what set of thoughts would make me happier and sleep better.

You can write down or think about your own three things that you can use before you go to sleep at night:

1. I'm so grateful for…

2. I'm grateful to live…

3. I am a successful…

There are certain things that I don't always say to myself such as:

- I am a great Dad.

Or

- I am a good runner.

The reason for this is because those things are already part of who I am, so my subconscious mind already believes it.

In other words, there is no need to convince myself that I need to become it, because I live it.

You'll find that it's the same with you.

There are certain things that you know that you're good at, and you don't have to spend any conscious time trying to convince yourself that you are good at it.

You just are!

What you say to your loved ones before you go to sleep will also make a big difference.

What do you think I say to my son before he goes to sleep?

I always say words to Léon such as:

- My champion.
- World's best Son.

And

- Love you Léon.

When I do this, he goes to sleep knowing that the person closest to him (along with his Mum) believes in him and loves him.

So, just to summarise, when you're sleeping, your subconscious mind is working away, and your subconscious mind will work either for you or against you!

CHAPTER 4

GET ENOUGH SLEEP

"Sleep is the best meditation."
– Dalai Lama

The two important questions here are:

1. How important is it to get the right amount of sleep?

2. How much sleep do we need?

The answer to question one is extremely important!

The second question isn't quite as easy to answer, as there are many different factors that will determine how much sleep you need, age being one of the main ones.

Obviously, babies and children need a lot more sleep because they are in a rapid growing phase.

I was listening to Arnold Schwarzenegger one day on the Tim Ferris Podcast, and he said something very much in line with my own thoughts on how much sleep we need.

Arnie said when he was in his late teens he would need around 9 hours sleep, but now in his later years, he usually sleeps for 6 hours and that's enough for him.

At the age of 46 (at the time of writing) I also sleep for around 6 hours and find that's enough for me, but it can also go up to seven or eight hours depending on how badly I need it.

However, the age and the time we should sleep for isn't the same for everyone.

There are no exact rules to follow for how much sleep you should get as everybody is different.

What is very important is to get enough sleep so that you feel refreshed in the morning, and you can go out and have a really productive day!

I remember when I was in the Army (and maybe still now for some people) you would hear things like, "you can sleep when you're dead," which was basically making reference to getting by on less sleep, so you could spend that time working on a goal.

If that is what you want to do then that's fine, as long as you don't go through your day saying things like, "I'm so tired, I've been up since 5am, 4am, 2am" or whatever else it is.

Some people like to try and impress others by saying how early they get up, how late they go to bed and how busy they are, which is something I personally get bored of hearing.

"Oh so you haven't had much sleep, would you like a medal for that?"

"Oh so you're really busy? Join the hundreds millions of other people all over the world that are also busy."

When it comes to some of the highest achievers in the world of health and fitness, such as Olympic athletes or sports stars, you will hear some of them talk about how important getting the right amount of sleep is for their training.

When it comes to finances, the richest man in the world, at the time of writing, Jeff Bezos, is reported to sleep a good eight hours a day!

Just to put a final nail in the coffin that sleeping for only four or five hours a day will make you more of an achiever in life; Albert Einstein was reported to sleep for around 10 hours a day!

One of my major goals in life was to have a lifestyle in which I could sleep as much as I wanted to and get up whenever I wanted.

Although I'm lucky enough to live that life now, I still remember what it was like to wake up to an alarm for at least five days a week.

I can't say that it was something I enjoyed; however, it was necessary at the time to get by until I reached my goal of getting up when I wanted to.

If you're dragging yourself out of bed in the morning then you probably need more sleep, so you'll have to make a conscious effort to go to bed earlier.

I know it's not rocket science is it?

However, when we have a goal to hit, or there is some sort of deadline hanging over us, sometimes we have to put in the late hours and get the job done.

The question we have to ask ourselves is, "how important is it to reach my target in relation to the quality of my life and my mental health?"

If you are staying up late some nights to hit goals, and you don't manage to get your full sleep in, it's not the end of the world.

However, if you're doing this night in, night out for months on end, then it'll have a negative effect on both your mental health and your body.

When I don't get enough sleep, I start to get agitated at minor distractions, which hinders my creative thinking and process for writing and production.

Think about how you function when you haven't had enough sleep.

One of the masters of ancient Greek literature 'Homer' said it best:

"There is a time for many words, and there is also time for sleep."

According to Oxford University sleep expert Professor Colin Espie, most people are not getting enough sleep. Professor Espie states:

"The importance of sleep for individual and societal benefit has been almost completely neglected in both policy and practice."

A report that Professor Espie helped to put together called, 'Waking up to the health benefits of sleep', for the Royal Society for Public Health, stated that the UK public is under sleeping by an average of almost an hour every night.

Which over the course of one-week is one whole night worth of sleep deprivation!

The Royal Society for Public Health's study of 2000 UK adults revealed:

- Average sleep time is 6.8 hours, which is below the average of 7.7 hours that most people feel they need.

- 54% of the people in the study felt stressed as a result of poor sleep.

One part of the study certainly increased my level of happiness and made me laugh when it stated:

- One in 20 people have fallen asleep during sex.

Of course you can't simply say that everybody has to have eight hours of sleep and that's the end of the conversation.

Some people won't want to sleep for eight hours; whereas other people feel that they need more than eight hours of sleep to function at their optimal level.

Ultimately, you will know if you're getting enough sleep because your own body will tell you.

If you're tired and stressed all of the time then you'll have to go to bed a little bit earlier.

The argument against this is that you need to do your work, you need to spend time with the children, you need to do exercise, you need some of your own time, and you also need time for your relationships with people.

This is true for many people, but if you're going through life like a walking zombie, then you're going to have to make getting enough sleep a priority!

If you have to cut 15 minutes off your exercise routine, cut 15 minutes off spending time with a loved one, cut 15 minutes off not spending time with the children or cut 15 minutes off just having some time to yourself, then do it!

However, also find the balance in all areas of your life, rather than cut any areas down too much, or out completely.

Do it for your own sake and for the sake of people around you, because the better you feel, the better your attitude towards others will be.

Of course, this is a complete generalisation, and some people won't have children, or family members, or they won't want to spend any minute of the day on their own, or they don't do any exercise.

All of that is irrelevant.

Ultimately, what this shows is, whatever you put your time into, you can always cut down certain activities so that you can get an hour more sleep if you feel you need it.

With 24 hours in the day you could say that 6 to 8 of those hours is for sleep, maybe there is eight hours of work and maybe there is eight hours after work until you go to bed.

Again, this is different for everybody.

Some people will want to sleep less, and some want to sleep more.

Some people will want to work more, and some people will work less, and of course, some people will have more free time than others.

People that know me well, know I'm a pretty driven person, but that doesn't mean I'm on the go all the time with lots of energy and enthusiasm.

I also have days where I think, "I can't be bothered to do anything and I'd like to just chill in the garden, on the sofa or lie down on the bed, and maybe read something or watch a movie."

You have to be driven to achieve things, but sometimes you just need to take some rest time and go again when you're feeling fresh.

You'll hear many times throughout some of my books that it does take extra effort to be successful in life, but you have to know the difference between productive extra effort and burning yourself out, in which you're constantly tired and operating on only 80% capacity.

If you're not getting enough sleep and you feel tired all day, you simply won't enjoy life as much, you won't be able to make smart decisions like you can when you're fully recharged and you won't be happy.

Ultimately, make it a priority to get enough sleep because it will lead to a happier and healthier life!

"Sleep is that golden chain that ties health and our bodies together."
– Thomas Dekker

CHAPTER 5

START YOUR DAY OFF RIGHT

"Happiness depends upon ourselves."
– Aristotle

When NASA launches a rocket, they will have put a lot of thought and preparation into it. Also, when they launch the rocket it needs to be going in exactly the right direction.

If a rocket is destined for deep space (which is a starting point of 2 million kilometres away) and is only 1 degree off at the start of its launch, by the time it reaches deep space, it will be thousands of miles off course if it is left unadjusted.

It's important that we start our day off right because the better we start our day off the more likely we are to keep on track with being happy throughout the day.

As we go through our day there will be little challenges that come up that can, if we let them, throw us off course.

So, we need to be constantly adjusting, we need to focus on the big picture and the end goal, while at the same time enjoying all the little things around us that we can be grateful for.

I woke up one morning and was thinking about things that didn't go right for me in the past, which of course is never a good way to start your day.

You may have also done this yourself several times in your life.

As I stood there in my home, I thought, hang on a minute; life is perfect for me right now.

I thought about the present moment:

- I wasn't in any physical pain.
- I had food in my belly.
- I had enough water to drink.
- I was with my son Léon.

So, I changed what I was saying to myself in my head, from what I haven't got, to what I have got, and of course it made me feel better!

You may be in a dark place and think that you haven't got much going for you.

You may be so focused on what you haven't got that it's clouded your reality, and you can only see the negative things in your life.

If we want to be happy, it's vital that we don't focus on what we haven't got and focus on what we have got!

These could be things like:

- Your family.
- Your health.
- The country you live.
- The time in history you live in.

Think about and write down 10 things that you have got in your life right now:

- ....
- ....
- ....
- ....
- ....
- ....
- ....
- ....
- ....
- ....

Out of these 10 things, which ones could you take out of your life?

Probably not many of them!

So, appreciate them, cherish them, and think about how lucky you are to have certain things in your life.

If you take living in your country for granted, or if you think that people or the government of your country has wronged you in some way, then how would you like to be exported to places such as:

- Iraq
- Afghanistan
- The Congo
- Rwanda
- Sierra Leone

If you're not bothered about the time you live in, let's transport you back to:

- The Dark Ages
- The Stone Age
- World War 1

If you don't care about where you are and the freedom you enjoy, let's transport you back to a place or a time that would have a negative effect on you such as:

- Being a slave
- Nazi Occupation
- Being accused of a crime you didn't commit and sentenced

It's always important to be grateful for what you've got!

FEED YOUR MIND WITH POSITIVITY IN THE MORNING

One of the things I've noticed over the years is that sometimes I'll be playing a self-development audio and one of my friends, girlfriends or family has heard it and thought that it's a waste of time and all a bit stupid.

Not all high achievers listen to self-development audio or read books, so you don't have to do it to be a success at something.

However, when you go outside of your own beliefs and thoughts, and start listening to other people's experiences and views on things, you then get a much broader perspective of life's situations and it can open your mind up to new possibilities.

Now, this next sentence may seem like bragging, but it isn't, all it is is something I've observed over the years.

The one thing I have noticed with the people who usually shun this habit is that I've never met one of these people who has better mental health than me or are happier than me.

They may be a lot more successful than me in different areas of their life, but in terms of happiness, definitely not!

Some of them may have achieved more in terms of medals or money but most of them seem to struggle more with day-to-day life.

I do know people that are very happy with their lives, but these people don't shun any type of psychological research or personal development.

In every case I've come across, the people that I know that are the happiest have educated themselves throughout the years on the inner workings of the mind, which means they are ahead of 95 to 99% of the population when it comes to mental toughness, happiness and overcoming challenges.

Am I saying that the happiest people I know (myself included) have got everything worked out in their minds and that their minds don't bat an eyelid when things go wrong?

Definitely not!

However, reading and listening to self-development material does give you the ability to bounce back far quicker than you would without it!

> ***"He who learns but does not think, is lost! He who thinks but does not learn, is in great danger."***
> – Confucius

CHAPTER 6

YOUR HAPPINESS DEPENDS ON YOUR FOCUS

"Happiness depends more on the inward disposition of mind than on outward circumstances."

– Benjamin Franklin

Some people love to wallow in self-pity and get into the habit of having self-defeating emotions every day.

It's much easier for them to wallow in self-pity than to make the effort to pull themselves out of the psychological hole in which they find themselves in!

Even though most people like this won't admit it, they end up in love with feeling sorry for themselves.

At the very least, they are more comfortable in their unhappiness and self-pity, than they are with making a positive change.

Most humans have gone through exactly the same types of feelings, emotions, and negative thoughts, such as feeling:

- Physically in pain
- Psychologically in pain
- Like a loser (when I'm not where I think I should be in life)
- Not loved
- Not wanted
- Rejected
- Lonely
- Sad
- Depressed
- Peeved
- Annoyed
- Pissed off
- Angry
- Jealous

- Wanting revenge
- Unforgiving
- The sense of loss
- Pathetic
- Weak

As well as a whole range of other negative emotions throughout our lives.

Yep, I've been lucky enough, or unlucky enough to experience a broad range of emotions, as I'm sure you have too?

This is good news, because if I was the sort of person that was just happy from the day I was born and nothing ever affected me emotionally, then it would be impossible for you to relate to me, or this book.

We're all human beings, we're all in the same boat together, and the vast majority of us are all built with these of emotions.

Despite having experienced these negative emotions, we can still develop our brains to minimise the affect of these thoughts, and we can subsequently recover a lot quicker by being more aware of them than when we were younger!

Most humans have also gone through exactly the same types of feelings, emotions, and positive thoughts, such as:

- Healthy
- Happy

- In love
- Loved
- Cared for
- Looked after
- Wanted
- Accepted
- Forgiving
- A winner
- Sympathetic
- Empathetic
- Generous
- Mentally strong

The chances are that you're just like me and you've been through pretty much all of these experiences too!

"Regardless of your circumstances, how you feel is mainly down to you, and what you focus on!"

If you're always focusing on the first negative list then you're going to make yourself depressed, but if you choose to focus on your wins in life, and the positive things in your life, whether they are in the past, present, or possibilities for the future, then you're going to be a lot happier!

Most people know that when you feed your body with things that are either high in bad saturated fats or things with a lot of sugar in them, then it's going to have a negative effect on your body in one way or another.

Even if you have one of these metabolisms where you can eat what you want and not put on fat, eating unhealthy food and drinks will have negative effects on your internal body systems.

How you look at things in life will make a massive difference to your happiness!

I was listening to a great audiobook by James Clear called 'Automatic Habits' and he mentioned that he had heard a story about a man who used a wheelchair and was asked, how does he feel using the wheelchair, because it confined him.

The man replied by saying that it doesn't confine him, it liberates him, as without the wheelchair he would be stuck at home all day and would not be able to get about as much.

Because that was the story he told himself, it made his life a lot easier as mentally he felt better about his situation, which in turn turned him into a happy person.

So, whatever your situation, you need to find a story that eases the mental strain in your head.

One day my son Léon asked me the question, "are you rich Daddy?"

It was a good question, and I had a good think about it before I answered him.

Of course the greatest wealth is your internal wealth, and how good your state of mind and mental health is; but I knew what he meant, so I answered him in terms of money.

I said, "It depends who you compare me to."

Léon replied, "What do you mean Daddy?"

"Well if you compare me to some people I'm not financially rich, but if you compare me to those children in Africa on the TV who are drinking dirty water, I'm extremely rich financially."

I was referring to an advert we had just seen on the TV where the actor, Jeremy Irons, was asking people to donate £3 to Water Aid by sending a text.

I remember listening to a Billy Connolly interview in which he said, "I know billionaires who don't think they're rich."

So, it's all down to how we look at things, and it's always better to focus on the positive than it is to belittle yourself or tell yourself what you haven't got.

Maybe there has been a time in your life when you felt secure in your job and then one day you got told that you were no longer needed… "Hasta la vista baby!"

You think, "oh great, now how am I going to pay for my food, my rent, my mortgage, my car, the gas, the electric, the loans I have?"

It's natural to think about all of those things and you may feel worried.

But we have to remember that,

"It's us that control our thoughts, not the events that happen to us!"

We can decide to interpret situations to our advantage.

I remember losing my job one day and I remember thinking, "shit, I've got no cash!"

But rather than worry myself or my family about what I didn't have, and what I had just lost; I decided to look at this as an opportunity.

In challenging times we need to ask ourselves the right questions.

In a situation like this, a good question to ask yourself is, "have I got more qualifications, wisdom and knowledge now than I did when I left school?"

If the answer is yes, then you have a massive advantage over when you left formal education!

You may say, "but now I have more bills to pay and responsibilities than I did than when I left education."

This is probably true, but would you rather go back to having what you had when you left school?

Many people would not.

On a personal note, I wouldn't like to go back to being 16 again.

Don't get me wrong, I'd like another 30 years extended on my life, but I wouldn't like to have to start from scratch all over again.

I wouldn't have the self-confidence that I now enjoy today.

The great experiences that I have had would not be there.

My knowledge would not be there, and my son would not be here.

Yes, there are other things that would be there, my grandad and uncle (that brought me up), my Siberian Husky 'Hope' would be there, heck even my hair would be there!

All jokes aside, there are certain things in life that we cannot change, and we have to be grateful for the time we've had with the special people in our lives.

Relationships will come and go, that is the natural way of life.

Whether somebody is taken from us because the relationship has ended, or on not such a great note or whether that person has passed away, people will disappear from our lives.

When I look back at some of my relationships with past girlfriends, rather than being bitter about them, I chose to be grateful for the time I had with them.

At the time of writing (June 2020) I've had five serious relationships in my life: Jo, Laura, Hayley 1 (my Son's mum), Hayley 2, and Ambreen.

Although a few of them may not have ended great (as happens sometimes) I still care about them all and hope they live a great life.

The way I look at things is, when one door closes, another one opens.

Never let bitter feelings consume you because by holding onto bitterness and negative feelings, the only person this will hurt is you.

As the Buddha said,

"Holding on to anger is like grasping a hot coal with the intent of throwing it at someone else."

Around 50% of marriages fail, and even the ones that don't end up in divorce, it doesn't mean that those couples have a fantastically happy marriage.

God knows how many relationships fail and over 70% of businesses fail, so if you try something and it doesn't work out, then don't worry. You're not alone!

Just because the thing you tried failed, doesn't mean you're a failure!

When adversity hits, you can look at it in the 'poor me' way, or you can think about what a great opportunity it is to show the world that you're a winner, no matter what happens!

I never look back at a job I didn't stay in, or a relationship I didn't stay in, as a failure.

Each one was a success for a certain period of time and I'm grateful for everything that I've experienced.

How do you think that affects me mentally?

It's pretty obvious, it makes me very happy, and you can do exactly the same thing too.

If you want to live the happy and fulfilled life you want, the only way forward is to focus on the positive things in your life!

CHAPTER 7

MAKE PEOPLE HAPPY

"Try to be a rainbow in someone's cloud."
– Maya Angelou

Making other people happy can add to your own happiness, but it's important you are also happy.

If you are making a lot of other people happy and you feel empty and unhappy in yourself, then it's because you're focusing on what you think you're lacking or you're not grateful for.

As Dodinsky said,

"Be there for others, but never leave yourself behind."

One day, I was sitting in my car outside the supermarket waiting for my mum to come out and I noticed a lady who was smiling, laughing, and interacting with other people.

This lady wasn't stunningly beautiful, in fact she didn't even have the best physique, but what she did have is an incredible personality.

As I watched this lady at the checkout I thought to myself how wonderful it was as I could see that she was a ray of sunshine in what is normally not the most joyous of places.

I thought to myself how grateful I am to have people in my life who are happy and make me feel better.

In life you can get two types of people.

1. The type of person that brightens up the room when he or she walks into the room.

2. The type of person that brightens up the room when he or she walks out of the room.

It's important to make an effort (because sometimes it does take an effort) to have a positive effect on other people's lives.

Nobody wants to be around doom and gloom all the time because it will drag you down as well!

When you go out of your way to pay a compliment to somebody or to try and lighten up somebody's day, you make a difference in a person's life.

The chances are if it's a stranger, you won't know what's going on in that person's life, but everybody in life is fighting a battle, and some are fighting harder battles than others.

Even as I sit here writing these words, a man rode past me in his wheelchair, and I can see that he is in his 70s, and he has only one leg.

As he goes around the back of my car, another car is blocking my view so I can no longer see this elderly gentleman in the wheelchair.

I decide to go out and see if I can help with anything, but fortunately somebody is already there and looking after him.

At some point in our lives we are all going to need help from people.

It doesn't matter if you're super-duper tough, or you're worth billions of pounds.

At some point, you will need somebody else to take the load off of your day.

We can't be there for everyone, but we can help some people some of the time.

When you make a difference in other people's lives you may not think much of it at the time, but the more you can make a difference in other people's lives, the more value you add to the community, and the more your own self-worth will grow.

As Martin Luther King Jr said,

"Life's most persistent and urgent question is, what are you doing for others?"

Whilst I was waiting again outside the supermarket and jotting down my thoughts, I had a little tap on my car. When I looked up, I could see Helmut, a local taxi driver looking at me and smiling.

Helmut's originally from Germany and when we met, we started talking about what a beautiful place Germany is as several years before, I had been to a part of Germany called Bavaria to visit the Neuschwanstein Castle.

Neuschwanstein Castle is a beautiful fairytale type looking palace that the Chief Designer at Disney, Herbert Dickens Ryman, is said to have modelled the Cinderella's Castle in Disney's Magic Kingdom from.

Helmut asked me how things were going, and I told him overall they were going really well, even though I had just broken up with my girlfriend.

"Oh" he said, and then went silent.

After somebody says words like that about a relationship break-up, with a boyfriend or girlfriend, the other person expects something negative to come out of your mouth.

However, I replied that I had parked my car down at the supermarket carpark so I could just watch hot girls go in and out all day long!

Helmut didn't expect me to say that and he burst out laughing!

Of course, I was just saying it for a joke, okay I was kind of half-joking but seeing him laugh also made me feel better.

As our conversation carried on, he told me that he loved seeing things that I had been doing for certain people.

So, I had made him feel good by complementing the country that he came from, and also by telling him that I was now the town's local pervert looking at beautiful women.

Helmut also made me feel good by telling me about the other good things I had been doing in the community.

The point of the story is, if you go out of your way to help people and make people feel better about themselves, the chances are they will return those feelings back to you.

Of course there are times when you are nice to people and they are not nice back, but most of the time, if you send good vibes out to people, then good vibes will come back to you.

You've probably done the same sort of thing yourself.

You've probably complimented someone and made them feel good, and in doing this, you feel good about yourself.

Even if they didn't compliment you back on something that you had done, there is a very good chance you would still have enjoyed sending out positive vibes to them.

So make others happy and it will help make you happier!

"Spread the love everywhere you go. Let no one ever come to you without leaving happier."
– Mother Teresa

CHAPTER 8

THE HAPPIEST COUNTRIES

Right, it's time to get political! Nah, only joking, but it needs to be said that Governments too can play a part in our happiness because laws and legislation affect our lives.

- Freedom
- Wealth
- Starting wars
- Poverty
- Ethnic cleansing
- Communism
- Democracy
- Taking responsibility and control of your life

I'm not going to go into the politics of the list above because that isn't what this book is about.

All I'm going to do is point out a few things that governments can control to various degrees.

In 2017, a report was published listing the happiest countries in the world.

The world happiness report ranked countries on six different factors, they were:

- Freedom
- Caring
- Generosity
- Honesty
- Income
- Health

Norway came out top!

Many experts believe that it came out on top because of high life expectancy, high levels of gender equality, very good healthcare, high GDP per capita, very good education and not to mention it's beautiful landscape!

Author and columnist Eric Dregni lived in Norway for one year and studied there for three years.

After he heard about the list, he decided to go back to Norway, talk to people and see if he could find some clues as to why as a nation, they seemed to be happier than most.

Dregni said, "Inger Brøgger Bull, a librarian from Oslo, didn't understand why Norway was ranked as the happiest country in the world."

She said, "we have bad weather, the highest prices for beer, things are so expensive!"

However, it turns out that Norwegians use the word 'we' a lot more than they use the word 'I.'

In many societies around the world it's more about 'ME, ME, ME' and what can I achieve, whereas Norwegians in general, focused more on everybody doing well in life!

For me, this was an important part of the survey and it meant a lot to me, simply because I have a very similar mindset, and I do sincerely believe that helping other people and caring about them plays a massive part in my happiness.

Even when people don't like me, or don't want me to do well, I still wish them all the best!

I know that sounds a little bit crazy, but the way I see it is, people have to deal with their own problems, and I haven't got time to worry about what they are thinking about and it should be the same with you.

If you worry too much about what people think about you, it can be detrimental to your happiness.

What people think about you has no direct effect on the way you feel and think if you decide to not let it bother you!

(I cover this more in my book 'No F*cks Given' which is due to be released in the later part of 2020).

One Norwegian also said,

"I think perhaps we Norwegians have become a bit smug, since we consider ourselves so peaceful and helpful. It's not so nice when Norway considers itself a bit better than other places."

When I read that paragraph I had to question it, because what's wrong with considering yourself peaceful and helpful?

I can see why the Norwegian said, 'we may be a bit smug about that,' but my feelings on it personally, is that he should be proud of that.

"If you consider yourself more peaceful and helpful than

the majority of people, then that makes you a better person, which in turn will make the world a better place."

As I continued to read the article, his wife Inger said,

"Openness to helping others is the essence of Norway's success. We have a willingness to give a part of ourselves for the whole."

That's powerful stuff!

Some of the other things on the list that many Norwegians considered valuable was being free in nature.

Everyone has a right to roam free in Norway!

According to the documentary, no one 'absolutely' owns the land, which means anyone can come and camp on people's land for the night, and all that is expected of you is to clean up at the end of your stay.

This is obviously a little different to many countries, as farmers wouldn't take too kindly to a lot of people camping on their land.

I have a scenario in my head of an angry farmer chasing a happy hippy weed smoking camper with a pitchfork!

I think back in the day, some farmers would have come out brandishing their 12 bore shotguns!

Employers in Norway are required to give employees at least

25 days of paid annual holiday, and they want their employees to enjoy it.

Even though Norway hit the top of the list in 2017, when I first researched this piece the country that had won the 'Happiest Country in The World' title the most times was Denmark (at the time of editing in 2020).

Ultimately, it's the Scandinavian countries that always rank highest in the World Happiness Report.

When it comes to paying taxes, 9 out of 10 Danish people will say that they are happily paying their taxes because they know it is going to benefit not only themselves, but also their community and their friends.

Norwegians trust their government to spend their taxes in ways that will hugely benefit the country and their community.

It seems that many Danish people are happy because they have guaranteed free child day care, free health care and a top-notch education system.

One of the main reasons for the higher overall happiness in Scandinavian countries, is that they are grateful for what the have got.

There's that word 'grateful' again, that seems to pop up all the time when it comes to happiness.

When I went to Denmark, I visited Copenhagen.

Copenhagen is one of the worlds most environmentally conscious cities, in which over a third of people ride bikes.

Rates of poverty, unemployment and homelessness are extremely low.

In Denmark, most schooling is free (which is the same as many rich countries) and when Danes go to university, they get some money to contribute towards their undergraduate education.

An American reporter visited Denmark and asked a Dane called Peter Morgensen a few questions.

Morgensen is an economist and chief political editor of Denmark's second largest newspaper, Politiken.

The reporter asked him, "How many Danes experience financial distress, or lose their homes, or go bankrupt because they get sick?"

Morgensen gave the American reporter a puzzled look and said to him, "why none of course" (because of government support for people).

The Dane was genuinely baffled by the question, because to him, it was ridiculous to think that anyone would lose their house or go bankrupt because of medical bills.

The reporter explained to Morgensen that every year millions of Americans lose their homes or go bankrupt because of medical bills.

The reporter went on to say that half of all bankruptcies in the United States are caused by people being sick.

Morgensen also told the reporter that in Denmark they couldn't imagine living like that.

The American reporter went on to say that one of the big reasons that the Danish are happier than Americans (in this example) generally, is because the Danish government supports parents massively when they have children.

American women receive an average of 10.3 weeks for maternity leave.

In Denmark, new mothers receive an average of 52 weeks parental leave and their salary paid for by the government (which obviously came from the taxes that most Danes happily contributed towards).

The rest of the paid time off can be divided by the family.

Denmark also consistently ranks as one of the best countries in the world for gender equality.

The gender pay gap is also substantially less in Denmark than in the US.

In Denmark, the gap between the richest people and the poorest people is one of the smallest gaps in the world.

The reason for the low levels of inequality links to the fact that the average middle-class Dane pays (at the time of writing) between 45% and 53% in taxes, while the wealthiest Dane's pay over 60% in taxes.

The poorest Dane's that are payed under $31,000 a year pay 30% taxes.

According to many surveys, Denmark has the best work/life balance in the world.

Social problems and bad health are far worse in countries with less equality.

In almost all the statistics from infant mortality, to mental illness, to teenage pregnancy, and to murder; it seems that the more equal a country is, the level of crime is lower, mental illness is lower, along with a whole list of other things.

Scandinavians generally take things in their stride far more than many other nationalities. Especially, a lot more than people who live in busy cities and succumb to 'the rat race', you know, the people who haven't got the time to talk because they're too busy being quote/unquote "busy."

One of the other things that stood out in the reports was that Scandinavians have a general respect for their fellow citizens.

In other words, they treat other people like they would like to be treated.

Scandinavians also have a very strong belief in the power of their community.

European countries such as Sweden, Austria, Switzerland, Germany, Norway, Luxembourg, and Denmark are not only normally in the top 10 happiest places in the world, but they also consistently rank in the top 10 countries in the world with the lowest crime rates.

I've been lucky enough to travel to all of those countries I just mentioned, and there is no doubt that I felt completely safe wherever I was.

America is one of my favourite countries on this earth, however there are so many places in America where you wouldn't find me in the early hours of the morning, simply because it's too dangerous.

Although much of western media reports that Africans are poor but happy, the reality is a little different.

I've been to Africa and I can say that I've met many happy Africans, but in general most of them would rather be in a country like the UK or other 'developed' countries.

In 2020, the happiest country in the world for the world happiness report was Finland.

Even though it fluctuated from country to country such as Norway, Denmark, and Finland one thing is pretty clear for us to see.

Every country that has topped the world happiness report is a Scandinavian country.

People in the UK can look at their country and think to themselves, but we have the biggest empire in history, we've got all of the most glorious kings and queens.

The Romans can look at their proud history and the Americans often come and say that they live in the greatest country in the world.

The reality is quite different on the world level though.

When you say your country is the best, or you are the best, our ego or patriotism takes over.

Many people are blinded and just believe what they hear.

There is nothing wrong with being proud about your own nationality. I'm incredibly proud to be British, and I wouldn't change it for anything.

I love our heritage, our history, many of our great leaders and high achievers, our National Health System, and our democracy.

There is so much that I love about living in Great Britain.

However, I do believe that a 'we' culture, like that of Scandinavia, is a more natural way of dealing with the stresses and strains of daily life!

Ultimately, no matter what country we live in we have to do the best with what we've been given and be grateful for it.

CHAPTER 9

THE HAPPIEST ENVIRONMENT

"You become like the five people you spend the most time with. Choose carefully."

– Jim Rohn

Several years ago when my son Léon was younger, I came across one of the 'Mr Men' books and thought it would be a good idea to introduce Léon to some of the 'Mr Men' characters.

As a child I had many fun memories of being read to or reading 'Mr Men' books.

Some of my favourites were 'Mr Happy', 'Mr Strong', and 'Mr Tickle' so I decided to buy a 'Mr Happy' book for my son and read it to him.

So the story goes a little bit like this:

One day, 'Mr Happy' goes for a walk and comes across a tree with the door.

He opens the door, walks down a set of stairs, and opens another door.

And what does he find when he's opened the other door?

He finds someone who looks exactly like him!

Yes, a big round, yellow looking human/creature or whatever you want to call 'Mr Happy's' character.

However, there was one significant difference between this character and 'Mr Happy,' and that was, rather than smiling, this character had a very unhappy face!

It was 'Mr Miserable!'

'Mr Happy' then asked 'Mr Miserable,' "how would you like to be happy just like me?"

And not in exactly the same words, 'Mr Miserable' says something to the effect of, "yeah I'm up for a bit of that!"

So 'Mr Happy' decides to take 'Mr Miserable' from his house and takes him to where he lives, 'Happy Land.'

After a while of living in Happy Land, 'Mr Miserable' gradually started to smile and become happy himself.

'Mr Miserable' even started to laugh, which in turn, made 'Mr Happy' laugh too.

'Mr Miserable' and 'Mr Happy' then went outside and continued to laugh until their sides hurt, they laughed until their eyes watered and they just kept on laughing.

When other people passed them by, it would make them laugh too.

Shit, even the birds in the trees started to laugh!

Well, I'm sure that you felt all warm and gooey inside about that beautiful little story didn't you?

But all jokes aside, the great thing about this little story is that there is a lot of truth to it.

If you're in an environment where you have consistently been unhappy, then you need to take your ass out of that environment!

You not only need to take yourself out of that environment, you need to be around happy and positive people who can lift your spirits; when you do that, you will indeed become a happier person!

However, you have to decide to be happy!

If you consistently want to be a grumpy bastard, and that is the vision you have of yourself, and that is the life you want to lead, then fine, you can stay grumpy.

Some people are happy being grumpy. Sounds a bit weird, but these people seem to enjoy being a grumpy and unhappy person because it's what they are comfortable with.

The most important thing is to be around good people who add some positive value to your life.

It's not just about associating with high achievers, because some high achievers may have a completely different set of values to you, and if that's the case, it would be soul destroying to be around people (no matter what their status), who do things that you feel very uncomfortable with.

You need to be around happy positive people, who like to help others and haven't got the world's allocation of dramas in their lives.

You've probably come across this type of person before.

Everything that happens in their lives is blown out of all proportion and boy do they like to have a song and dance about it!

You know it's the type of person who always says, "I don't suffer fools gladly."

Little do they realise they only need to look into the mirror to see who the real fool is.

They are the type of person who is operating on a very low level of consciousness, in other words, they can only ever see things from their perspective and to hell with how you feel.

They also like to play the victim in life all the time, if you've had it tough, they've had it tougher, and they'll be the first person to tell you about it!

If you have this type of person in your life, then your life is going to be a pile of dramas and very unpleasant situations, in short…your life will be a pile of shit.

It doesn't matter how healthy you are, it doesn't matter how much you achieve, it doesn't matter how much money you have, if you're around this type of person long enough, they will turn your life into a steaming pile of cow poop!

We all know someone like that, but if you've got this type of person as one of your friends, and you're in touch with them every day, then I suggest you back off and spend your time somewhere else.

If your partner is this type of person and won't change their ways, that's like them being the iceberg and you're the Titanic.

In other words you're heading for a crash and you'll be on the way down if you don't change course.

I don't care how positive or how motivated you are, if you're around a poisonous person all the time, your mental state will take a turn for the worst.

I can't stress enough how important it is to be around the right people!

CHAPTER 10

BEING KIND TO PEOPLE

"Be kind, for everyone you meet is fighting a hard battle."
– Plato

The type of people that I like the most are the ones that are down-to-earth and kind to people.

They treat people as they would like to be treated.

When you're kind to people, the chances are, they're going to be kind back to you.

However, this doesn't always work in life.

Sometimes, you get people that want to take advantage of your kind nature; I know first-hand, as years ago I got bullied a bit.

I was never nasty to those people or rude to them, but they decided to take it upon themselves to be complete twats to me!

Looking back, maybe I should've just hit the person and win or lose, it could have stopped their bullying, which is what I did with somebody when I was around 16 years old.

The guy kept on punching me in the arm for no reason and giving me a nasty look, and this happened several times until I got to the stage where I'd had enough of it and told a friend that I was going to have a fight with him.

My friend went and told the bully that I said I was going to fight him, so the bully decided to come over to me, grab my hair and say, "I hear that you wanted a fight with me?"

I knew that I might as well just go for it, so I dropped the head on him and fortunately won the fight.

He never bullied me after that.

That challenge with the other bullies was that it was mainly in army training, and I was scared of getting thrown out of the service.

They were both a higher rank than me and loved by the Sergeant who was also a complete asshole and a bully!

I was classed as a 'nobody' back then in my troop and if I got kicked out for fighting it would be no loss to anyone apart from myself.

My confidence was very low back then, and I thought that if I was kicked out for fighting, I'd struggle to get another job, and my life would be one massive struggle and completely boring.

Some people that are bullied can turn into bullies themselves but doing that always works against you in the long run.

Being kind is the way ahead not only for other people, but for us too!

Just doing little things like letting somebody out when they're stuck in traffic, or holding the door open for somebody, will make that person happier and you should also feel good for doing it.

I was staying in a hotel one evening and as I was walking

through the reception area, on the way to my room, I noticed an intoxicated woman being extremely rude to one of the male receptionists.

He had done nothing personally wrong to gain the wrath of this woman; all he had done was be in the wrong place at the wrong time.

Later on that evening, I ended up going back to reception when the woman had gone.

I had a chat to the guy at reception and said to him, "don't worry about that she's just had too much to drink and none of that is your fault."

I could see that he was still a bit shook up by the whole situation, and I wanted to do something that would help counter his negative feelings.

I needed my clothes ironed for the next day so I asked him if he could bring an iron to my room and I also asked if he could bring some sweeteners as well for my coffee.

Within the next 5 to 10 minutes he came up with the iron and the requested handful of sweeteners.

I thanked him for this, and I said to him, "do you believe that out of every bad situation comes a positive situation?"

He wasn't from the UK, and I didn't know how well he spoke English, but he kind of looked on in bewilderment at my question, so I said to him, "I believe that good things can come from negative situations," and with that, I went over to my desk in my room got a £10 note and gave it to him as a tip.

He said that there was no need to give him a tip, but I just said take it and have a great evening.

I could see that he appreciated the tip and I knew that it was a ray of light on his dampened spirits.

In all honesty I can say that I felt quite good for giving him the £10, but at the same time I did think to myself it's not about how I feel, my main goal was to make him feel a little bit better and a little bit happier.

If you can be a ray of light in somebody's life, whether it's a small gesture or something big, it can really make a difference to people's lives!

There's no losing in a situation like this, the chances are, you'll feel good about what you've done, and the chances are, they're going to feel a little bit better about you having come into their life and showing kindness towards them.

If you want to gain more happiness in your life then it's always a good idea to make other people happy.

However, there are some people who make other people happy that aren't happy themselves.

A typical example of this are some comedians.

There are many comedians out there who make it their life's

work to lighten peoples load in life and make other people happy through their comedy.

Sadly, some comedians hit some very dark times.

Of course there are a couple of obvious people that we can think of, one being Robin Williams, who sadly took his own life.

Jim Carrey also went through a time in which he was very depressed and struggled with life.

So, making other people happy doesn't always make yourself happy, this goes back to the thoughts you say to yourself.

Being more famous or having more money doesn't necessarily create happiness, as we know.

There are countless examples of celebrities that have gone through a very dark period in their lives.

If you were to ask me which one book I consider the best book I've ever read in my life, the book that really comes to mind is Dale Carnegie's, 'How to Win Friends and Influence People.'

Getting on in this world has a lot to do with how well you get on with other people, and if you're looking for a book on how to master people skills, be influential and get what you want then this is a great book to read.

When it comes to getting certain things in life, it's always a good idea to give before you receive.

One of the things I always try to do to the best of my ability is to give value to other people.

Even with this book, I want to give value, and even if just one sentence in this book helps you in some way in life, I know that this book will have achieved its purpose.

Many authors have a dream of being a bestseller, which is cool and everything, but for me, it's never really about that, it's more about helping people in some way.

Yes, all of these other achievements and accolades are always a nice little bonus but for me, it's not the main purpose of this book.

One of the little side bonuses of helping a person is it can be very beneficial to your mental health.

Many people know that exercise is an excellent way to feel good about yourself and stay positive, but sadly, all too often these days, the doctor will prescribe pills for somebody who's feeling down and going through a bad patch. In my experience however, we need to try other options first.

I haven't covered exercise in depth in this book because it's something that I'll cover in other books.

One of the major benefits of being nice and sincere to people is it is very good for your mental health.

If you're a bit rude and arrogant, sometimes that can come back and bite you on the bum.

It might even get to the stage when you think 'poor old me.'

However, you may be able to trace your behaviour back and see that you caused a lot of the problems that you now have.

"Three things in human life are important.
The first is to be kind.
The second is to be kind.
And the third is to be kind."
– Henry James

CHAPTER 11

YOUR PERSONAL CHEERLEADERS

"No individual can win a game by himself."

– Pele

An experiment conducted by a TV show called 'Brain Games', on the National Geographic Channel, showed a woman who tried to get a basketball through a net and was given 10 shots.

There was also a crowd of approximately 15 volunteers standing and watching her.

When she started missing the shots, the crowd sent out negative vibes towards her.

The first time she attempted the 10 shots she didn't score any baskets and felt emotionally deflated, as not only was she missing the shots, but the crowd were not supportive and very dismissive of her.

She was then blindfolded, and while standing at the same place where she previously shot from, she tried to score two baskets with two shots with the blindfold on.

However, the difference was this time, she had a crowd there cheering her on.

When she threw the first ball, the crowd cheered and told her she had scored a basket (when in reality, the shot was way off the basket).

Of course, she was delighted with this so, still blindfolded, she tried with a second shot, and again, the crowd cheered her as if she had scored a basket twice in a row which lifted her spirits massively!

She believed she was scoring baskets even though she wasn't!

She was feeling pretty good about herself at this point and was asked to take another 10 shots without a blindfold on.

This was the same as what she had first done, but this time the crowd were totally behind her and really supportive, even when she missed the basket.

She missed the first shot, and she also missed the second shot, but the crowd was still totally supportive of her.

Even though she was missing the basket, she was a lot closer to scoring than when the crowd wasn't supporting her.

On her third attempt, she threw the ball and it went straight through the net.

Everybody, including herself, was delighted with this and it gave her a huge psychological boost!

On her fourth attempt, she threw the ball and it hit the rim of the basket, not once but twice, and then incredibly, the ball bounced through the net!

Again, she was delighted!

The crowd had big smiles on their faces; they were clapping their hands and were showing total support for her.

The Presenter of Brain Games said afterwards:

"Wow! By making her think she sank those blindfolded shots, and by cheering and giving positive reinforcement, it's almost like we hacked her self-confidence and got her to believe more in her natural abilities."

Amazingly, she scored 4 out of 10 baskets, which was a huge improvement from her 0 out of 10 shots.

They also conducted another experiment in which they got a good basketball player, called Josh, who (not blindfolded) scored 9 out of 10 baskets.

The experiment wanted to know if there was anything that the people around him could do to make him a worse player.

Josh then had to put a blindfold on and was asked to take one shot.

When the presenter said to the crowd, "do you think he can do it guys?"

The crowd replied very negatively and said, "no."

Josh had a smile on his face even though the crowd responded negatively and then stood at the line ready to throw his first shot blindfolded.

When he took the shot he missed it, but (unlike the crowd from the girl that wasn't as good with her initial shots), the crowd sent out negative vibes his way.

The negative vibes weren't aggressive, but they were very unsupportive, and he knew they didn't believe that he could do it.

The TV presenter said to him, "not quite, but it's okay, let him try a second time."

Josh threw the second shot, again he missed, and again the crowd sent out negative vibes, booed and said "no."

In all fairness, from the outside Josh still had a smile on his face and didn't look too discouraged.

The presenter then asked Josh to take off his blindfold and said,

"So listen, it wasn't as easy as we thought, but let's have you do 10 throws again without the blindfold. Do your thing, 9 out of 10, maybe 10 out of 10."

As Josh stood to throw his first basket the crowd still weren't supportive of him, and when they were asked by the presenter if they thought he'd get a basket, they said "no."

Josh threw the first shot and scored a basket, but even though he scored, the crowd was still negative and booing.

At this point, you could see that the crowd had got to Josh mentally!

On the second shot, the crowd were booing him, and Josh missed the shot with the ball bouncing off the outer rim of the basket.

Josh was still smiling, but you could see that he was also deflated.

On his third shot, he missed again, whereas before without the crowd's negativity, he scored 9 out of 10 shots.

On the fourth attempt, he also missed and fell short!

The crowd kept saying negative things and in the end, Josh only made 5 out of 10 baskets, which was four down from his average before.

Josh was very good compared to the average person; he certainly wasn't a professional but the negative people around him severely affected his performance!

They did 'the positive crowd' and 'the negative crowd' experiment on many other people and for the most part the result was the same.

When people were supporting and cheering the person trying to score the basket, the player performed on a higher level; when the crowd were negative and unsupportive, the players generally performed on a poor level!

However, there were a minority of people that still managed to score high on a consistent level even when the people were booing and unsupportive of them.

When they were asked how they had the ability to do that, one of the women said that she used to play college basketball and was used to people booing and reacting in a negative way.

In other words, she had trained her brain to a higher level and part of getting to that higher level was focusing and not being rocked by the negativity that was around her!

Most of the best professional basketball players will focus so intensely and believe in themselves so much, that even if the crowd were booing them, they would still perform at a high standard!

But this can affect professional players too.

If you've ever watched any sports match on TV, you'll know that when a team plays a home game they are more likely to win.

Yes, they may be more familiar with the ground, but even more important than that is the support from the fans, which gives them more of a psychological boost and helps them perform better.

In fact there are many high achievers that use this negative psychology to spur them on.

Michael Jordan was arguably the greatest basketball player in history. He was one of these people that used negativity from others to drive him on mentally to help him become the success that he was.

Whenever Michael Jordan had bad press or somebody would personally challenge him, he would rise to the challenge and make a point of thrashing the pants off them!

In fact, people that knew Michael, always said that you

should never challenge him, because the chances are, he's going to kick your ass!

We need to do the same thing in life!

Many times there will be the naysayers and doubters in your life, but rather than let that affect you in a negative way, use it as fuel to succeed!

I can tell you from personal experience that I have a lot of people that want to see me go down in flames, which has ironically made me succeed more in life!

So, if I can make that happen, you can too!

However, Michael and other professional team players still have a team around them and fans around them that want them to win.

So, if you have someone that is constantly tearing you down and not supporting you, then you have to make plans to remove them from your life before they grind you down with their unsupportive, negative bullshit!

"Get around people that support you."

With some people, you can give them a pass once or twice if they've been through a difficult situation and said some unkind things to you.

However, it's best to play it like a yellow card if they are constantly nagging at you or being horrible in some way.

If this continues for a long enough period of time, eventually, you need to give them a red card so that they're out of your life!

Most of the time, a substitute will come in and fill the gap in your life that the negative person left, but even if they don't,

"You are strong enough to go forward without them on your own!"

CHAPTER 12

BEING GRATEFUL

"Do not spoil what you have by desire in what you have not; remember that what you now have was once among the things you only hoped for."

– Epicurus

Roman statesman and philosopher Marcus Tullius Cicero (more commonly known as simply 'Cicero') who was one of Rome's greatest orators, described 'gratitude' as the 'mother of all human feelings!'

And according to positivepsychology.com

"It is not happiness that brings us gratitude. It is gratitude that brings us happiness."

There is also peer reviewed scientific research that shows that gratitude actually does the following things to our bodies:

1. Releases toxic emotions

2. Reduces pain

3. Improves sleep quality

4. Aids in stress regulation

5. Reduces anxiety

6. Reduces depression

Léon once said to me, "Daddy would you sell everything in this house for £50,000?"

I stopped and thought about it for a few seconds and said, "I wouldn't sell you."

He said, "No, I mean all of the things in the house like the TV, the laptop, the iPad, the phones etc."

Of course this was quite easy to decide, as every item was not worth as much as £50,000 so I would've gone with the £50k.

However, if somebody offered you £50,000 to get rid of your phone, laptop, tablet, TV, bed, chairs, forever and you could never have them back and you couldn't replace them, would you do it?

Many people, including myself wouldn't.

The reason being, on a personal note, if I got rid of my Samsung smart phone, my iPad, my laptop, and my TV etc, it would be much more difficult to do my work and I could spend the £50k in a relatively short space of time.

Also, to be without a phone or the other devices that we enjoy everyday is something that most people (unless you're a hermit living in a cave) wouldn't opt in for.

I talk about being grateful in some of my other books and I will continue to talk about it in future books too! The reason? Because

"Being grateful is everything when it comes to happiness!"

In fact if you're not grateful it's very difficult to experience true happiness.

In 2013, I moved into a spacious house with my girlfriend in one of the nicest areas in town.

My fitness training was almost non-existent I just did a few bits here and a few bits there.

I had a fairly good income, with a nice sports car and a fast motorbike parked in the drive.

I got comfortable and was drifting along in a fairly easy job. I worked as a support worker and did things like take people with epilepsy, brain injuries, learning difficulties, and autism to the cinema and played games of pool and went for walks with them.

I was a nightclub bouncer, which was also pretty easy.

Most of the time was spent watching people and talking to people every now and again, and every so often, myself and my fellow bouncers would break up a fight.

When I worked in the pubs there wasn't fighting guaranteed on a weekly basis, but in the nightclubs, it was kicking off more often than not.

My other job was doing a little bit of personal training, which normally involved running or power walking.

It's so easy to get caught up in the whole yeah but I'm too fat, too broke, too ugly, too old, too young, not smart enough, not tall enough, not short enough, I don't have the contacts etc…

It's true that there are certain things you're born with that you may not be able to change, but your thinking isn't one of them! So, feed your mind with positive thoughts.

Feed it with fun, with laughter, with inspiration, with quality people, who will genuinely build you up!

So, always visualise yourself being successful because you already are successful at many things.

Think about all of those people that are actually dying from starvation and other diseases that the super rich people in the western world don't have to worry about.

When I say super rich, I mean someone that earns about £10,000 a year, because that is super rich compared to several billion people around the world!

In the UK we've got it even better to some extent in that, you can walk through a wooded area or you can lift up a piece of wood without worrying about a snake biting you and killing you!

After all, we don't have to worry about deadly spiders or frogs, or alligators and crocodiles seriously screwing up your day!

There are no dingoes to take our babies away, no wolves to hunt us down, no lions and tigers and bears 'oh my' that will maul the living crap out of you!

I was lying in bed next to a girlfriend one evening and she read out a quote from a fairly well known entrepreneur who rose to prominence over the past few years through his YouTube channel and the global publication of his books.

The quote was a good one, but one of the things I've noticed about certain people in the quote/unquote 'world of personal achievement' is some (but not all) take themselves and life far too seriously!

Of course when you want to achieve certain goals you have to take them seriously, but when all that matters is the next goal, the next award, or the next mighty dollar then it's easy to stop enjoying life and stop being grateful.

I've seen many people get so consumed in achieving their goals, regardless of anything else, that they risk losing any form of fun in their lives!

Some people have a belief that everyone should follow 'their way' and with that, the fun can vaporise for them too!

As a result, those that develop this tunnel vision will go on to suffer from mental health issues like, stress and anxiety.

So, no matter what goals you are achieving, have fun and be grateful for what you have got!

CHAPTER 13

MONEY MONEY MONEY

"Happiness resides not in possessions, and not in gold, happiness dwells in the soul."
– Democritus

If happiness is all about getting 'things' then everybody in the western world should be ecstatic because what we have compared to billions of people in developing countries is quite shocking.

There are many millionaires that are happy and live a very gifted life. But I'll never forget meeting a guy who told me he was worth £3 million but all he wanted was £6 million.

It's always cool to be striving for new goals, but when your happiness depends on that goal you aren't heading down a dark path, you're already in the dark!

You must decide to be happy right now:

- Not when you become single
- Not when you've got the perfect partner
- Not when you get a divorce
- Not when you get married
- Not when the children leave home
- Not when you have children
- Not when you retire
- Not when you get a new job
- Not when you leave your job
- Not when you've hit a certain fitness goal
- Not when you lose a certain amount of weight
- Not when you put on a certain amount of weight
- Not when you have a certain amount of cash in the bank
- Not for any reason

DECIDE TO BE HAPPY RIGHT NOW!

You can have it two ways: you can be happy now and strive towards your goal, or you can be unhappy until you reach your goal of weighing a certain amount or having £6 million in the bank, like that guy I spoke to.

Ironically, he didn't realise that when he finally hits his target of £6 million he will probably be happy for a few minutes and then be unhappy because he wants £9 million to make him happy.

It's quite funny when you think about what he's doing; it's not that he's stupid, it's just that he's lost track of what success really is.

Most people believe that people's happiness and the quality of their lives boil down to monetary wealth. There is no doubt that money can help you greatly in your life, but the quality of your psychological wellbeing is not down to how much cash you have in the bank.

There are people who live in the slums of Mumbai who are not happy, there are people in the developed world, who are financially rich in comparison, that live an average life and are not happy.

There are also millionaires and billionaires who are not happy.

By the same token, there are people who live in the slums and people in the developed world who live an average life, as well as millionaires and billionaires who are happy.

I interviewed multimillionaire Alfie Best and asked him if money makes you happy. Alfie is a Romani gypsy that has built up his caravan park empire from nothing.

The last estimated value of Alfie's net worth was over £300 million.

Alfie replied that money can give you a level of comfort, but it doesn't make you happy all the time.

Money can move you to a better neighbourhood, away from people who bring drama into your life and it definitely gives you a lot more options.

So, have you ever thought that where you live can have an impact on your happiness?

In the UK, there was a popular daytime TV show called 'The Jeremy Kyle Show'.

The producers for the show would find people from the lowest income areas and invite them to become guests in exchange for talking about sleeping with their partners sister or their husbands Dad, or whatever else the crazy ass situation is!

The truth is that in many (but not all) low-income areas, there is more crime, there are more challenges, more mental health issues, more depression, and also more drug use.

One of my heroes in the personal development world was Zig Ziglar.

He was 'a good ol' boy' (as he would have described himself) from Alabama.

Zig was overweight and struggling in life and through the power of changing his mindset, he became one of the most successful self-development authors and motivational speakers in the world.

I have seen how people in the self-development industry and high achievers from all different walks of life, can become such workaholics that their work comes before anything else in life.

Trying to find a balance between making enough money for your family and spending enough time with your family can be a challenging thing to do.

Only a very small percentage of people seem to pull off making good money and spending enough time with loved ones…Zig Ziglar was one of those people!

I remember listening to a speech he did where he said that he was not the best motivational speaker in the world because if he put that much time into speaking, it would come at a high price, and that price was not investing time with his family.

For me personally, it put him in a higher league than many speakers and authors who are constantly on the road chasing the money and recognition at the expense of not seeing their family, or at the expense of not having downtime on their own, or with friends and loved ones.

There is a danger that by being so focused and obsessed with a certain goal, you can lose something far more important – time with the people you love and truly care about!

Although I have many ambitions and goals, I'm also aware that I need to have a balance and it's something I recommend you keep an eye on with your own life too.

If you have the mindset that you'll be happy only when you've got a certain thing in your life, whether that's a handbag, a car, a new man, a new woman, a boat, a watch, a holiday, you're literally wasting your life. You're wasting Life!

I'm not dismissing getting things either, because certain things can make you happier.

For example, if you really enjoyed whatever product you bought then that's great, but your happiness shouldn't depend on these material things!

Getting additional 'things' should just be a tiny little bonus.

When I was a child, I used to love playing with toys such as my 'He-Man' figures or 'Star Wars' models.

I used to love going out on my bike, and I would put a little piece of cardboard next to the spokes with a peg on the bike's metal frame, so that it would make a sound like a motorbike.

Of course it didn't sound exactly like a motorbike, but it was as close as I was going to get at 5 years old.

Think back to when you were younger and what you enjoyed doing.

What 5 things can you think of?

1. ....

2. ....

3. ....

4. ....

5. ....

If you can't afford certain things, then you can always find many things that you can enjoy.

When I was in my junior school, I was quite content playing a game of marbles.

Or I'd play 'pitch and toss' with my friends, which is where you play for pennies and throw a penny next to a wall to see who gets closest to the wall. If your coin is closest you win.

If you were a real 'high-roller' you would sometimes play with a two pence or even a 5 pence piece!

Having money can definitely take some challenges away, but

it is not THE answer to total bliss, happiness, and fulfilment!

"It isn't what you have or who you are or where you are or what you were doing that makes you happy or unhappy. It is what you think about it.
– Dale Carnegie

CHAPTER 14

EXERCISE

"If you are in a bad mood go for a walk. If you are still in a bad mood go for another walk."
– Hippocrates

Hippocrates was an ancient Greek physician and was considered to be one of the most important figures in the history of medicine.

He is also referred to by some as the 'The Father of Medicine.'

Some have also credited Hippocrates with being the first person to believe people died of natural causes rather than superstition or the Gods.

Of course, you could still argue that it was God who put the disease into somebody's body, or it was God that sent the bus that knocked you down, but that argument is for someone else's book; and while that type of argument goes on about theories, I'd rather stick to certainties that can help you.

Anyhow, Hippocrates was rocking the scene from 460 BC to 370 BC.

He died at the grand old age of 90 years old.

Many people will live to 90 years old today, and actually, the average life expectancy, depending on which country you are born in, is closer to 80 years old in first world countries.

What was pretty outstanding about Hippocrates, was not only his vast knowledge as a physician; he also survived for so many years at a time when people usually kicked the bucket at a much younger age than they do today.

An article published in 'Scientific American' said that we are now living in an era where three generations coexist, which is called the evolution of grandparents.

Whereas, in some eras of human history, three generations would not have existed, and the grandparents would've died at a much younger age.

In other words, Hippocrates knew his stuff and was a big fan of exercise!

By now we should all know many of the benefits of exercise, so you may think there's no need for me to go on about them, but I will.

Not to teach you something you already know, but to reinforce what you probably know anyways so that it can motivate you to do some form of exercise.

And the sooner you do it, the more benefits you will reap.

You may be reading this book at 11pm and might be thinking about going to bed.

But why not do 5 press-ups (or whatever number you can do) before bed?

Many people think doing five press-ups is insignificant and it will not make a difference.

They may also think that just going for a 400-metre walk is totally insignificant, but if it's 400-metres more than you did yesterday, or the day before, then it is significant!

Why?

Because you're making progress!

It's the same with the press-ups.

If you did 10 press-ups today, and you never did 10 press-ups yesterday, you're making progress!

So, the goal is to simply do a 'little bit more' than you've done before.

When it comes to happiness, it's more about taking action and getting into the habit of doing some form of physical exercise, than it is achieving some massive feat of human endurance.

There are so many people in this world today with mental challenges, heck let's face it, we all have mental challenges at one time or another!

Whether that challenge comes from the loss of a loved one or it comes from physical pain, which also has an effect on the mind.

But before we go reaching for pills from the doctor, the best thing to do is some form of exercise.

The renowned Harvard Medical School did a report several years ago on the benefits of exercise.

Some of the benefits are:

- Stress Reduction
- Anxiety Reduction
- Helps Fight Depression

The website www.womansday.com says, "exercise not only changes your body, it changes your mind, your attitude and your mood. Exercise should be regarded as a tribute to your heart. Good things come to those who sweat."

You probably don't need me to tell you this, but if you exercise on a regular basis and eat a balanced diet then, chances are, you're going to be a happier person overall.

At the end of the day, yeah it's all about taking action!

Reading words in a book is one thing but putting those words into action is where people who are struggling become winners in the game of life!

Apart from numerous studies that have been done on the benefits of exercise and how it helps happiness, from my own personal experience, I know that after I've exercised I always feel better for having done it.

I not only feel better for having done it, but in doing it my body is able to be in better working condition. As a result it's going to be more efficient with daily activities like walking up stairs or carrying things.

Exercise also keeps my body fat down and this gives me a

psychological boost.

There is nothing wrong with being overweight if that is how you want to live your life.

Frankly, it's none of my business how you live your life, and there are many people out there that are confident, happy and big, which is all cool by me.

I'm just one of those people that enjoys the benefits and the results of exercise.

Love it or hate it, when it comes to having a better state of mind and better mental health, exercise makes the difference!

EPILOGUE

It's worth mentioning again, that finding happiness is, in one form or another, in all of my books.

This book serves as only a brief, but I hope, important guide to you finding more happiness and living a better life.

When all is said and done, no matter

- What country you live in.
- What race you belong to.
- What your beliefs are.
- Whether you're a man or a woman.

None of it ultimately matters!

What does matter is

"It's up to us as individuals to decide whether or not we are going to be happy!"

Too many people wait for happiness, too many people pursue happiness.

Happiness is a state of mind and to a great extent, you CAN control your thoughts!

DECIDE TO BE GRATEFUL FOR WHAT YOU HAVE AND BE HAPPY NOW!

ACKNOWLEDGEMENTS

It's almost impossible to say how many people have helped me along the way with producing this book, and if you're not in the acknowledgements just know that I am very grateful for your support and help.

However, I would like to say a massive THANK YOU to a few people that I can think of, off the top of my head:

My Mum – Diana Beckerleg, 29 Commando Regiment, Royal Artillery, 3 Commando Brigade and The British Army.

Tom Webb, Paul 'The Viking' Hughes, Thomas Hughes, Eva Savage, Mark 'Billy' Billingham, Julie Colombino-Billingham, Tracy, Maria and Kay Morris, Cheryl Hicks, Jamie Baulch, Gene Hipgrave, Kauri-Romet Aadamsoo, Mark Dawson, Craig Martelle, Michael Anderle, James Blatch, Michael and Emma Byrne, Paul 'Faz' Farrington, Des, Paul Heaney, James Atkinson, Des Powell and Laura Taylor.

Also, a huge THANKS to 'The Mark Llewhellin Advance Reader Team' for taking the time to read the manuscript and make suggestions.

ABOUT THE AUTHOR

In 1990, Mark Llewhellin left school without knowing his grades. He had little confidence and was not at all optimistic about his future.

Not knowing what to do with his life Mark followed some of his friends into the Army. He failed his basic 1.5-mile run, was bullied, and was also voted the fattest person in the Troop!

After a year with the Junior Leaders Regiment Royal Artillery, Mark decided he would try and get into 29 Commando Regiment Royal Artillery, which is an elite Army Commando Regiment that at the time proudly held the Military Marathon World Record (i.e. a marathon carrying a 40lbs backpack).

After failing the 29 Commando Selection phase (called 'The Beat Up') twice, first through lack of fitness and secondly through an injury, Mark subsequently passed on his third attempt and completed the 'All Arms Commando Course' on his first attempt.

Mark later went on to achieve the following:

- Break the 100-kilometre Treadmill World Record.
- Place 1st in the Strava Distance Challenge in 2015 competing against over 51,000 runners.
- Place 1st in the Strava Distance Challenge in 2014 competing against over 40,000 runners.
- Run and walk 70-miles without training on his 40th birthday.
- Become a successful Personal Fitness Trainer.
- Complete the Marathon Des Sables (a six-day, 135-mile ultra-marathon in the Sahara Desert).
- Work and live in London's exclusive Park Lane as a Bodyguard.
- Run 1,620 miles in the United States whilst carrying a 35lbs pack.

Mark has interviewed some of the world's top performers and high achievers in various locations, including one of the world's most prestigious memorabilia rooms…the Hard Rock Café Vault Room in London.

He has travelled to over 50 countries and has been featured in leading national newspapers and on TV for his running achievements.

Mark has extensively worked in the support and care industry for many years helping individuals with brain injury, autism, epilepsy, dyspraxia, and various types of learning difficulties.

He is the Managing Director of Mark 7 Productions, as well as the Producer and Host of 'An Audience with Mark Billy Billingham' speaking events around the UK.

Mark is currently working on more personal development books and lives with his son Léon (when Léon's not at his Mum's) on a beautiful marina in South West Wales.

ALSO BY MARK LLEWHELLIN

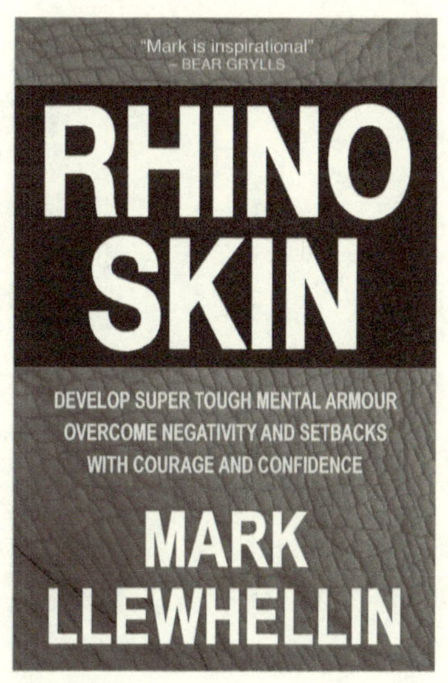

NUMBER 1 BESTSELLING AUTHOR

STAY STRONG

ELIMINATE NEGATIVE THINKING AND BECOME A STRONGER AND MORE POSITIVE PERSON

MARK LLEWHELLIN

"POWERFUL!"
Kate Strong – World Triathlon Champion

PUT YOUR BIG BOY PANTS ON

HOW TO MASTER YOUR MIND AND EMOTIONS
BUILD SUPERIOR MENTAL TOUGHNESS
THINK POSITIVE AND LIVE THE GOOD LIFE

MARK LLEWHELLIN

NUMBER 1 BESTSELLING AUTHOR

SMALL CHANGES
REMARKABLE RESULTS

TIME TO TOUGHEN UP

DEVELOP IMMENSE INNER STRENGTH AND CONFIDENCE
OVERCOME CHALLENGES AND ACHIEVE YOUR GOALS

MARK LLEWHELLIN

AN EASY GUIDE TO ACHIEVING YOUR GOALS
AND TRANSFORMING YOUR LIFE

JUST GO
FOR IT

NUMBER 1 BESTSELLING AUTHOR

MARK
LLEWHELLIN

Sign up for free at www.markllewhellin.com for offers, updates and new releases.

DISCLAIMER

Although the author and publisher have made every effort to ensure that the information contained in this book was accurate at the time of release, the author and publisher do not assume and hereby disclaim any liability to any party for any loss, damage, or disruption caused by errors or omissions in this book, whether such errors or omissions result from negligence, accident, or any other cause.

A Mark 7 Publications Paperback.

First published in Great Britain in 2021

by Mark 7 Publications

ISBN 978-1-914006-36-4

Book design and formatting by Tom Webb
pixelfiddler@hotmail.co.uk

IF YOU ENJOYED THIS BOOK

Your help in spreading the word about Mark's books is greatly appreciated and your reviews make a huge difference to help new readers change their lives for the better.

If you found this book useful please leave a review on the platform you purchased it on.

www.ingramcontent.com/pod-product-compliance
Lightning Source LLC
LaVergne TN
LVHW050920080826
845145LV00001B/141